ISHMAEL REED

a primary and secondary bibliography

A
Reference
Publication
in
Afro-American
Studies

Charles T. Davis, *Editor*
Henry-Louis Gates, Jr., *Associate Editor*

ISHMAEL REED

a primary and secondary bibliography

ELIZABETH A. SETTLE
THOMAS A. SETTLE

G.K.HALL &CO.

70 LINCOLN STREET, BOSTON, MASS.

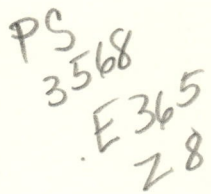

Library of Congress Cataloging in Publication Data

Settle, Elizabeth A.
  Ishmael Reed, a primary and secondary bibliography.

  Includes index.
  1. Reed, Ishmael, 1938-   —Bibliography.
I. Settle, Thomas A.   II.   Title.
Z8736.S46 [PS3568.E365]   016.813′54   81-20035
ISBN 0-8161-8514-X   AACR2

This publication is printed on permanent/durable acid-free paper
MANUFACTURED IN THE UNITED STATES OF AMERICA

In Memoriam

Louis Newton Bell

1940-1980

Contents

The Authors

Elizabeth Settle holds an MSLS from the University of Southern California and an MAEd in Instructional Media from California State University, Long Beach. She is the Chair of the Reference Services Department at California State University, Dominguez Hills, where she also teaches library skills and strategies. Her publications include bibliographies on musical comedy and reference sources in education, and numerous reviews for Preview Magazine and Choice.

Thomas Settle received his BA from California State University, Dominguez Hills, and his MBA from Pepperdine University. He has taught English at the University of Kansas. He has published articles on Henry Adams's novels, on the teaching of composition, and on prose style.

Foreword

Five years ago, a famous black critic called my editor and com-
plained about my book, <u>Flight to Canada</u>. He felt that the book was
too "bourgeois," and the characters "pathological." I'm fortunate
that his protests ended there, for if I were in a country where he
controlled the army and the police force, I would have been arrested,
or shot.

A month ago, I received a letter from a "feminist" scholar at
the University of Cincinnati, informing me that her choice of my
work as subject of her dissertation was "disputed" by the chairperson
of women's studies on the grounds that I was a well-known "sexist."
I recommended that the letter writer read this bibliography, compiled
by Elizabeth and Thomas Settle, in order to appreciate what critics,
who've not been content with single-phrased dismissals of my work,
have had to say about my books.

As a black male writer, fortunate enough to still be published in
a time when the media has created the image of black men as rapists,
muggers, and brutes--people are reluctant to share an elevator with
you--perhaps I shouldn't complain. Critics even write that I don't
have trouble being published, or that I can "write anywhere" I
please.

During the last five years, major essays and plays of mine have
been rejected on political grounds, and so, though I am pleased
that the critics in the following pages have devoted so much time to
my work--the list is as big as the personnel of a General Motors
plant--I am still conscious of the fact that I am a black male writer,
who is treated as shabbily as any other black male (until they find
out who I am), and that I am a member of a class which has been cast
to the bottom of the American caste system, and from those depths I
write a vision which is still strange, often frightening, "peculiar"
and "odd" to some, "ill-considered" and unwelcome to many.

The men and women in this bibliography have generally done their
best to grope with that vision. Maybe one day I can assemble them

Foreword

all in one room and buy them a drink or apple juice, or whatever
they prefer. I would begin the event with a toast to the Settles
for their patience, and the care with which they have put this book
together.

Ishmael Reed
December 1981

Introduction

Ishmael Reed's career still evolves. But his impact on American letters since his first novel, Free-Lance Pallbearers, has been immense, as evidenced by the mass of words devoted to his works. Reed, in his forties, is perhaps only in the middle of his career. He was born February 22, 1938, in Chattanooga, Tennessee. His first novel was published in 1967 and he has produced since that date five other novels, four books of poetry, edited two major anthologies, collected two books of essays, produced numerous reviews and critical articles, and served as editor of five issues of a major small multi-cultural press literary magazine. Reed continues to be a major literary leader of a third world press; he has in short been a very busy writer. One of his novels has been translated into French, Spanish, and Dutch, and all of his work is beginning to receive critical attention in Europe, Asis, and Africa. Throughout his already extensive works emerge the concerns of a writer who wishes to include the impact of Afro-Americans on the culture of the United States in the corpus of American letters. His tone and style are sometimes of satire and parody (though he employs as many techniques as are available to the writer), but his intentions are deadly serious, as evidenced by his numerous essays advancing his major contribution--the aesthetic of Neo Hoodooism.

In each of his novels, all of his poetry, and some of his essays, Reed tries to make new myths, explode old forms, exhaust useless stereotypes. His success can be viewed from the opinions of his peers, his reviewers, and the general literary establishment. The Reed criticism divides into several major categories. The first reviews his works and attempts to categorize him and his work along the more conventional lines of literature. Many of these reviews show the misunderstanding his world view has evoked. The second discusses the seriousness of Reed as a writer. The third phase, the one at present, gives consideration to Reed's total output, establishes his place in the Olympiad of literati, and examines the aesthetic vision of his prodigious outpouring. The real upswing in attention started with the publication of his third novel, Mumbo Jumbo, and has since settled into a more even tempo. Reed's publication history spans major houses and the minor houses, from Doubleday to NOK. Reed's works have been nominated twice for the National Book Award, once for poetry and once for fiction.

Reed has also encouraged the publication of many lesser known artists, particularly those who, like himself, are members of Third World peoples living in First World societies. They include Asian Americans, Native Americans, Chicanos, and Afro-Americans. His encouragement has ranged from inclusion in his various anthologies to the publishing of those works through his own publishing company, Reed, Cannon & Johnson. For his efforts, Reed has received several grants including a recent one from the California Arts Council to edit and publish an anthology of California poetry, Calafia. With the publication of Calafia, his latest work, Reed has begun to resurrect little known, and often forgotten, poets of the past. The impact of Reed's own poetry can be viewed from the vantage point of the numerous inclusions of his works in anthologies, including the Norton Anthology of Poetry.

This Reference Guide is organized along the lines of others in this series: entries are arranged chronologically. This format allows users to note the trends in the criticism of Reed as well as in to locate his primary works in order of their publication. The Guide covers the period from the publication of Free-Lance Pall-bearers to the present, roughly from 1967 through the end of 1980, though some entries from 1981 have been located. The Guide also provides a listing of Reed's poetry published separately as well as anthologies. Each annotation provides a combination of synopsis and pertinent quotations to reflect that author's view or evaluation, as we wish this Guide to be a contribution to the furthering of discussion about this controversial contemporary American author and his works. We have personally seen and read all materials for which annotations are provided. Works not actually examined by the authors have an asterisk immediately preceding the item number. "No pagination" at the end of a citation indicates that the item was obtained from a clipping service or examined in the form of tearsheets, etc., bearing no page numbers.

Two indexes conclude the Reference Guide. The index to works by Reed lists works by title (e.g., articles, poems, novels, anthologies, etc.), by editor and title of anthologies where his work appeared, and by significant mention of other authors or subjects in an article or review. This index is particularly helpful as it gives access to Reed's poetry and its subsequent reprintings in one source. The index to works about Reed enters the materials by author, title of work, and authors or titles which are significantly mentioned in the body of the review or article.

We heartily appreciate the work of Norma Carlsen of the Inter-Library Loan Department of California State University at Dominguez Hills for her invaluable work in helping us to obtain copies of materials. We also wish to acknowledge the assistance of the numerous University and other libraries who have helped in so many ways. And finally, we are most indebted to Ishmael Reed for allowing us to examine his papers.

PART ONE

Writings by Ishmael Reed

I BOOKS

<u>Novels</u>

<u>1967</u>

1   <u>Free-Lance Pallbearers</u>. Garden City, N.Y.: Doubleday,
      155 pp. 22 cm. First Edition.

2   <u>Free-Lance Pallbearers</u>. New York: Bantam Books, 116 pp.
      19 cm.

<u>1968</u>

3   <u>Free-Lance Pallbearers</u>. London: MacGibbon & Kee, 155 pp.
      21 cm.

<u>1969</u>

4   <u>Free-Lance Pallbearers</u>. New York: Bantam Books, 116 pp.
      18 cm.

5   <u>Free-Lance Pallbearers</u>. Toronto: Bantam Books, 116 pp.

6   <u>Yellow Back Radio Broke-Down</u>. New York: Doubleday, 177 pp.
      First Edition.

7   <u>Yellow Back Radio Broke-Down</u>. Garden City, N.Y.: Doubleday,
      "Limited Paperback edition." 177 pp.

<u>1971</u>

8   <u>Yellow-Back Radio Broke-Down</u>. London: Allison & Busby,
      177 pp.

3

1972

9   Mumbo Jumbo. Garden City, N.Y.: Doubleday, 223 pp. 22 cm.
     First Edition.

10 Yellow Back Radio Broke-Down. New York: Bantam Books,
     213 pp. 18 cm.

1973

11 Mumbo Jumbo. New York: Bantam Books, 256 pp. 18 cm.

12 Yellow Back Radio Broke-Down. London: Allison & Busby,
     192 pp. Second edition.

1974

13 Last Days of Louisiana Red. New York: Random House, 179 pp.
     22 cm. First Edition.

14 Last Days of Louisiana Red. New York: Avon Books, 191 pp.
     18 cm.

1975

15 Free-Lance Pallbearers. Chatham, N.J.: Chatham Booksellers,
     155 pp. 22 cm.

16 Mumbo Jumbo. Barcelona: Ediciones Grijalbo, S.A. Translated
     by Horacio Gonzales Trejo.

17 Mumbo Jumbo. Paris: Editions du Seuil. Translated by
     Gerard H. Durand.

18 Yellow Back Radio Broke-Down. Chatham, N.J.: Chatham
     Booksellers, 177 pp. 22 cm.

1976

19 Flight to Canada. New York: Random House, 179 pp. 22 cm.
     First Edition.

20 Flight to Canada. New York: Avon Books, 192 pp. 18 cm.

1977

21 Free-Lance Pallbearers. New York: Avon Books, 116 pp.
       18 cm.

22 Mumbo Jumbo. New York: Avon Books, 256 pp.

23 Yellow Back Radio Broke-Down. New York: Avon Books, 213 pp.
       18 cm.

1978

24 Mumbo Jumbo. New York: Avon Books, 256 pp. Second printing.

Essays

1973

25 This One's On Me. New York: Doubleday. Never published.
       Scheduled for August, 1973. Withdrawn in 1973.

1978

26 Shrovetide in Old New Orleans. Garden City, N.Y:
       Doubleday, 292 pp. 22 cm. First Edition. Retitled from
       This One's On Me.

1979

27 Shrovetide in Old New Orleans. New York: Avon Books, 332 pp.
       18 cm.

Poetry

1970

28 catechism of d neoamerican hoodoo church. London: Paul
       Breman, 28 pp. 22 cm. First Edition.
           Includes: "Black power poem"; "I am a Cowboy in the
       Boat of Ra"; "There's a whale in my thigh"; "Instructions
       to a Princess"; "the feral pioneers"; "Badmen of the guest
       professor"; "Sermonette"; "Dualism"; "catechism of d neo-
       american hoodoo church"; "Gris Gris."

1971

29   <u>catechism of d neoamerican hoodoo church</u>.   London: Paul
     Breman, 28 pp.   22 cm.   Second Edition.

30   <u>catechism of d neoamerican hoodoo church</u>.   Detroit, Mich.:
     Broadside Press Publications.

31   <u>catechism of d neoamerican hoodoo church</u>.   London: Paul
     Breman, 28 pp.   22 cm.   Third Edition.

32   <u>catechism of d neoamerican hoodoo church</u>.   London: Paul
     Breman, 28 pp.   22 cm.   Reprint of third edition.

1972

33   <u>Conjure; Selected Poems, 1963-1970</u>.   Amherst: University of
     Massachusetts Press, 83 pp.   24 cm.
       Includes: "The Ghost in Birmingham"; "The Jackal-
Headed Cowboy"; "The Gangster's Death"; "the feral
pioneers"; "Instructions to a Princess"; "There's a whale
in my thigh"; "I am a Cowboy in the Boat of Ra"; "Black
power poem"; "The Neo-HooDoo Aesthetic"; "Sermonette";
"Mo-jo Queen of the Feathery Plumes"; "The Black Cock";
"Betty's Ball Blues"; "The Wardrobe Master of Paradise";
"catechism of d neoamerican hoodoo church"; "why I often
allude to osiris"; "my thing abt cats"; "man or butterfly";
"hoodoo poem in transient"; "Monsters From The Ozarks";
"beware: do not read this poem"; "Dualism"; "Guilty, the
New York Philharmonic Signs Up a Whale"; "if my enemy is a
clown, a natural born clown"; "the piping down of god";
"Anon, Poster:"; "american airlines sutra"; "the inside
tract"; "for cardinal spellman who hated voodoo": "dragon's
blood"; "columbia"; "treatment for dance w/ trick ending";
"Back to Back: 3rd Eye"; "off d pig"; "General Science";
"Report of the Reed Commission"; "what you mean I can't
irony?"; "white hope"; "Untitled I"; "Untitled II"; "Untitled III"; "Untitled IV"; "Gangster Goes Legit"; "this
poetry anthology i'm reading"; "dress rehearsal paranoia
#275"; "Paul Lawrence Dunbar in the Tenderloin"; "from the
files of agent 22"; "introducing a new loa."

1973

34   <u>Chattanooga: Poems</u>.   New York: Random House, 55 pp.   22 cm.
     First Edition.
       Includes: "Chattanooga"; "Railroad Bill, A Conjure
Man"; "The Kardek Method"; "Haitians"; "Skirt Dance";
"Kali's Galaxy"; "Poison Light"; "The Decade that

Screeamed"; "The Katskills Kiss Romance Goodbye"; "'law
isn't all'"; "Antigone, This Is It"; "And the Devil Sent a
Ford Pinto Which She Also Routed"; "Cuckoo"; "Rock Me,
Baby"; "Mystery 1st Lady"; "To a Daughter of Isaiah"; "My
Brothers"; "The Vachel Lindsay Fault"; "Back to Africa";
"Swift, Tiny and Fine"; "Crocodiles"; "Al Capone in
Alaska"; "Visit to a Small College"; "The Atlantic Monthly,
December 1970"; "The Last Week in 30"; "Loup Garou Means
Change Into"; ".05"; "The Author Reflects on His 35th
Birthday"; "Jacket Notes."

1978

35   A Secretary to the Spirits. New York: NOK Publishers Inter-
national Ltd, 42 pp. Illustrations by Betye Saar.
Includes: "Pocadonia"; "Poem Delivered Before Assembly
of Colored People Held at Glide Memorial Church, Oct. 4,
1973 and Called to Protest Recent Events in the Sovereign
Republic of Chile"; "A Secretary to the Spirits"; "Sather
Tower Mystery"; "Foolology"; "The Return of Julian the
Apostate to Rome"; "Sputin"; "Sky Diving"; "Soul Pro-
prietorship"; "Vamp"; "Sixth Street Corporate War";
"Poetry Makes Rhythm in Philosophy"; "Untitled"; "The
Reactionary Poet"; "Rough Trade Slumlord Totem"; "Tea
Dancer Turns Thirty-nine"; "Memo to Stevie Wonder."

36   A Secretary to the Spirits. Lagos, Nigeria: NOK Publishers
Ltd, 42 pp. Illustrations by Betye Saar.

II EDITINGS

1967

1   The Rise, Fall, And . . . ? of Adam Clayton Powell. New York:
Bee-Line Books. (Managing editor.)

1970

2   19 Necromancers From Now. Garden City, N.Y.: Doubleday,
369 pp. 22 cm. First edition.

3   19 Necromancers From Now. Garden City, N.Y.: Anchor Books,
369 pp. 18 cm.

Writings by Ishmael Reed

1972

4   <u>Yardbird Reader</u>. Vol. 1. Berkeley, Calif.: Yardbird Pub-
      lishing Cooperative. (Editorial director.) First edition.

1973

5   <u>Yardbird Reader</u>. Vol. 2. Berkeley, Calif.: Yardbird Pub-
      lishing Cooperative. (Associate editor.) First edition.

6   <u>Yardbird Reader</u>. Vol. 1. Berkeley, Calif.: Yardbird Pub-
      lishing Cooperative. Second printing.

1974

7   <u>Yardbird Reader</u>. Vol. 3. Berkeley, Calif.: Yardbird Pub-
      lishing. (Editorial director.) First edition.

1975

8   <u>Yardbird Reader</u>. Vol. 4. Berkeley, Calif.: Yardbird Pub-
      lishing Co. (Editor-in-chief.) First edition.

1976

9   <u>Yardbird Reader</u>. Vol. 5. Berkeley, Calif.: Yardbird Pub-
      lishing. (Editor-in-chief.) First edition.

1978

10 <u>Yardbird Lives</u>! New York: Grove Press. (Edited with Al
      Young.) First edition.

11 <u>Y'Bird Magazine</u>. Vol. 1, No. 1. Berkeley, Calif.: Y'Bird.
      (Editor-in-chief.)

1979

12 <u>Calafia: The California Poetry</u>. Berkeley, Calif.: Y'Bird
      Books. (Project director.)

Writings by Ishmael Reed

III EXCERPTS AND SHORTER WORKS

1970

1 "Yellow Back Radio Broke-Down." The Spokane Natural 4
   (25 June):12.

2 "D Hexorcism of Noxon d Awful." In 19 Necromancers from Now.
   Edited by Ishmael Reed. Garden City, N.Y.: Doubleday,
   pp. 293-309.

3 "D Hexorcism of Noxon d Awful." Amistad I: Writings on Black
   History and Culture. Edited by John A. Williams and
   Charles F. Harris. New York: Vintage Books, pp. 165-82.

1971

4 "Can a Metronome Know the Thunder or Summon a God?" In The
   Black Aesthetic. Edited by Addison Gayle, Jr. Garden
   City, N.Y.: Doubleday, pp. 405-6.

1972

5 "Part I. Da Hoodoo. . . ." In Nommo: An Anthology of
   Modern Black African and Black American Literature. New
   York: Macmillan Co., pp. 414-23.

1973

6 "The Loop Garoo Kid." Cutting Edges: Young American Fiction
   for the 70s. Compiled by Jack Hicks. New York: Holt,
   Rinehart & Winston, pp. 436-50.

1974

7 "The Last Days of Louisiana Red." Ramparts 12 (January):
   28-30, 53-58.

1975

8 "Flight to Canada." Fiction 3, nos. 2-3:7-8.

9 "From Flight to Canada." Iowa Review 6, no. 2 (Spring):74-82.

10 "The Last Days of Louisiana Red." Players 1 (January):28,
    94-96, 98.

11   "The Loop Garoo Kid." <u>Superfiction or The American Story</u>
      <u>Transformed: An Anthology</u>. Edited by Joe David Bellamy.
      New York: Vintage Books, pp. 259-73.

1976

12   "Flight to Canada." In <u>American Poets in 1976</u>. Edited by
      William Heyen. Indianapolis, Ind.: Bobbs Merrill Co.,
      pp. 264-74.

1977

13   "From 'The Freelance Pallbearers': A screenplay." <u>Nimrod</u>
      21/22:214-25.

1978

14   "The Free-Lance Pallbearers." <u>The Seattle Review</u> 1, no. 1
      (Spring):7-11.

IV OTHER WORKS

Articles, Reviews, Interviews

1965

1   "Poetry Place: Protest." <u>East Village Other</u> 1, no. 1
     (October):5.
         Review of Carol Berge's <u>History of New York Coffeehouse</u>
     <u>Activities</u>. The style of the review shows Reed's early
     interest in orthography, later to be used in his novels and
     poems.

1966

2   "Villager Knifed Aiding Bar Patron." <u>East Village Other</u> 1
     (January):1, 10.
         Straightforward news story.

Writings by Ishmael Reed

1967

3 "The Black Artist--Calling a Spade a Spade." <u>Arts Magazine</u>
41 (May):48-49.
Directed at the "art establishment." It represents an
impassioned cry for black artists to have their chance.
Similar in style to his novels, this article seems most
clearly connected to <u>Mumbo Jumbo</u>. Reed reviews Archie
Shepp's play <u>Junebug Graduates Tonight</u> and gives painter
Joe Overstreet a pat on the back. "Part of the Doctrine,"
a poem by LeRoi Jones, is reprinted, and a prepublication
notice for <u>Free-Lance Pallbearers</u> is given.

1968

4 "Writing a First Novel." <u>The Writer</u> 81 (May):24.
Indicates that "the form of the novel is so elastic as
to enable the first novelist to do many 'untrodden'
things." Reed also notes that "technology, instead of
his curse, will be his boon. . . . today's novelist can
capture the diction and attitudes of a whole class merely
by tuning in 'Lucy' or 'The Honeymooners' or the fantas-
tical six o'clock news."

1969

5 "<u>Snaps</u> by Victor Hernandez Cruz." <u>East Village Other</u>,
19 March, pp. 17-19.
Reed gives enthusiastic notice to a new volume of poetry
by a young author. He views Cruz as "an original American
poet. He is young, together, and his work is heavy pagan
feet crushing the imperial dead (x's for eyes) metaphors,
allusions, symbols and images that characterize the American poetry establishment. . . . The most remarkable thing
about these poems are the nowness the newness the ownness
and the passion."

1970

6 "Can A Metronome Know the Thunder or Summon a God?" In
<u>19 Necromancers From Now</u>. New York: Doubleday, pp. 24-37.
Summary statement on why <u>19 Necromancers</u> was organized.
He advances the notion that "Thoth, the black Birdman of
Egypt, 'invented letters' and 'gave names to things'. . . .
the nineteen necromancers [are] of two worlds [who] do a
'speaking in tongues.'" The book represents "the new
Literary Neo HooDooism. Some plant their flags on things;

we plant our flags on the seventies." The essay is a con-
tinuation of Reed's evolving definition of Neo Hoodooism.

7   Introduction to 19 Necromancers From Now. New York:
     Doubleday, pp. xii-xxvii.
        An investigative criticism into the relationship of
     Afro-American literature and its place in the body of
     American literature. Reed relates some of his own expe-
     riences in major colleges with teaching Afro-American
     literature: "Students who would never think of turning a
     seminar on Melville into a political rally would not hesi-
     tate to dictate to a Black instructor what emphasis should
     be made or what works should be covered in his course."
     Reed concludes his essay with an attack on Marshall
     McLuhan's idea that "Words are 'oxcarts' and may disappear
     sooner than we think. . . . If McLuhan and [William]
     Burroughs had opened their reading to include the new
     Afro-American and Chinese-American writers, they would
     have found that print and words are not dead at all."

8   "Letters: Books in Black." Harper's Magazine 240 (March):6.
        Reed replies to Irving Howe's review of Free-Lance
     Pallbearers. Reed finds Howe out of touch with contempo-
     rary white writers, "let alone Black." Reed asserts that
     he intended his novels to be a "variation of Afro-American
     novelists Wallace Thurman and George Schuyler but it seems
     that Howe is illiterate of Afro-American literature written
     prior to 1938." He offers this opinion in opposition to
     Howe's suggestion that Reed intended his novels to be a
     black variation of Jonathan Swift.

9   "Neo HooDoo Manifesto." Los Angeles Free Press, 18 September,
     p. 42.
        A major statement which defines what Reed means by Neo
     HooDoo. "Neo HooDoo believes that every man is an artist
     and every artist a priest. You can bring your own creative
     ideas to Neo HooDoo." Reed also discusses other artists
     whom he considers to be Neo HooDooists. A portion of
     "catechism of d neoamerican hoodoo church" is included.

1971

10   "Born to Rebel: An Autobiography by Benjamin Mays." New
     York Times Book Review, 25 April, pp. 47-48.
        Reed reviews the book and finds in it a history of a
     man whose contributions to the black experience are sub-
     stantial indeed. Reed hopes that Born to Rebel will be as
     vigorously promoted as "the numerous volumes that demean
     the black experience." Reed notes, as does May, that the

historical struggle of blacks didn't just begin in the 60s
as is often presented by both black and white intellectuals.

11   "Ending the Western Established Church of Art." Essence 1
(January):15.
        Reed attacks the financial policies of "establishment"
art museums, music foundations, and other monied supporters
of the arts. He includes an excerpt from a document sent
to Senator Edward Brooke and Congressman Ronald Dellums
demanding changes at the Federal Government level. Reed
notes that many art pieces from Asia, Africa, and South
America were carted off to remote museums. His comments
on the "art establishment" are reminiscent of his section
in Mumbo Jumbo on "The Centers for Art Detention."

12   "Neo HooDoo Manifesto." Confrontation: A Journal of Third
World Literature 1: no pagination.
        Reprint of IV.9.

13   "Too Hot for Scanlans." Nickel Review (April):6-7.
        Explores what he sees as an historical process to rob
the black artist of his due place. Reed describes his
caricature of "Talking Androids" in Mumbo Jumbo. Several
photos depict the various approaches the media have taken
toward blacks, much in the style of Mumbo Jumbo.

1972

14   "Chester Himes: Writer." Black World 21 (March):23-38+.
        Reed describes Himes as "a great writer and a brave
man. His life has shown that Black writers are as heroic
as the athletes, entertainers, scientists, cowboys, pimps,
gangsters, and politicians they might write about."

15   "De Mayor of Harlem." Black World 21 (April):87-89.
        Reviews the book by David Henderson, contending that
Henderson employs "an aesthetic currently employed by
other contemporary Afro-American artists I would call Neo
HooDoo . . ." This review shows Henderson's connections
to Chester Himes and Zora Neale Hurston. The review
offers a clearly articulated expression of what Neo
Hoodooism is, and what force it can play in contemporary
literature. Reprinted in Shrovetide in Old New Orleans
(I.26).

16   "From Wood Carving to Bronze: A Conversation with Doyle
Foreman." Encore 1 (Spring):62-63.
        Reed interviews Foreman, finding him "the first real
Western documentary I'd seen and when he described the
land he sounded poetic." They talk about Foreman's craft

and art, his perceptions of the state of black contemporary art, and black arts in general. Reprinted in <u>Shrovetide in Old New Orleans</u> (I.26).

17 "Introduction I." <u>Yardbird Reader</u>. Vol. 1, pp. xix-xx.
A manifesto statement which outlines the reasons for forming the Yardbird Publishing Company run by "the victims [of callous publishers and editors]: writers, painters, sculptors, and their sympathizers in the fields of scholarship and business. We felt that our editorial and artistic judgment might be superior to our exploiters.'"

18 Introduction to <u>19 Necromancers From Now</u>. In <u>New Black Voices: An Anthology of Contemporary Afro-American Literature</u>. Edited by Abraham Chapman. New York: New American Library, pp. 513-524.
Reprinted from II.2.

19 "Neo HooDoo Manifesto." In <u>Conjure: Selected Poems, 1963-1970</u>.
Reprint of IV.9.

20 "<u>The Song Turning Back Into Itself</u>." <u>Black World</u> 21 (September):90-91.
Reed reviews Al Young's collection of poems and finds that Young is a new poet who achieves a full range of emotional feelings in his poetry rather than just the clichéd emotion of anger. Reprinted in <u>Shrovetide in Old New Orleans</u> (I.26).

1973

21 "<u>Before the War</u>." <u>Black World</u> 22, no. 4 (February):52, 74-75.
Reviews Lawson Fusao Inada's book of poems and finds influences of Afro-American culture in them. Reed praises the works as a peace-breaker, alluding to the quiessence of the Japanese-American community after their internment during the Second World War, finding that Inada has "broken the peace beautifully."

22 "Bird Lives!" <u>New York Times Book Review</u>, 25 March, p. 4.
In this review of Ross Russell's <u>The High Life and Hard Times of Charlie (Yardbird) Parker</u>, Reed finds some faults with both material included and some statements of Russell's, such as "I am annoyed when he [Russell] judges Louis Armstrong's music as 'archaic minstrelsy.' Such politically motivated statements deny an Afro-American musical tradition."

23   "George S. Schuyler Interview: Ishmael Reed and Steve
      Cannon." <u>Yardbird Reader</u> 2:83-104.
            An interview conducted in October of 1972 with Schuyler,
      who is "a distinguished journalist and is the author of
      <u>Black No More</u> (1931), the first science fiction novel writ-
      ten by an Afro-American." Reprinted in <u>Shrovetide in Old
      New Orleans</u>, (I.26).

24   "Gliberals." <u>New York Times</u>, 31 March, p. 35.
            Attacks the "white liberal establishment," and opts for
      the term "gliberals" to describe those of the establishment
      who seem to be moving to the right intellectually. Re-
      printed in <u>Shrovetide in Old New Orleans</u>, (I.26).

*25   "<u>Jumbish</u> by Elouise Loftin." <u>Washington Post</u>, 13 August,
      part B, p. 17.
            Cited in 1978.48.

26   "<u>Kulubi</u> by Edmund P. Murray." <u>New York Times Book Review</u>,
      7 October, p. 46.
            Reviews Murray's novel about Ethiopia and finds it
      biased. But since little news of Africa drifts across the
      Atlantic, "any information . . . is useful. Two stars,"
      insists Reed.

27   "<u>Music: Black, White, and Blue</u>." <u>Black World</u> 22, no. 6
      (April):79-81, 97.
            Praises Ortiz Walton's book as a milestone in musical
      criticism. Reed is particularly pleased with the treatment
      of American classical music (Afro-American contributions to
      American music). Reed finds Walton "has done his HooDoo
      work" and that it is a book which "can't be recommended too
      highly." Reprinted in <u>Shrovetide in Old New Orleans</u>,
      (I.26).

28   "A Westward Movement." <u>San Francisco Examiner</u>, 20 May, no
      pagination.
            Outlines the move by major Afro-American literary
      forces from New York to the Bay Area. Reed notes those
      Bay Area trends are already well-established on the West
      Coast, and includes mention of writer Cleo Overstreet.
      Reprinted in <u>Shrovetide in Old New Orleans</u>, (I.26).

                              <u>1974</u>

29   "Blacks Must Put 'Filthy' Money To Work." <u>Los Angeles Times</u>,
      26 December, Section II, p. 7.
            An article adapted from a speech Reed gave to the Con-
      ference of Black Writers at the Institute of the Arts and
      the Humanities at Howard University in Washington, D.C.

Reed essentially argues for massive financial support to the arts and the establishment of an Afro-American cultural bank which would "finance plays, films and publishing houses or buy time on television and radio or space in newspapers to be used in the common interest (of black artists and intellectuals)." Reprinted in Shrovetide in Old New Orleans, (I.26), with the title "Image and Money."

30   "Letter to Roger W. Gaess Concerning the Literary Achievements of Walter Lowenfels." Small Press Review 6, no. 3 (5 March):5-6.
    Reed finds it's "hard to write about Walter," but praises Lowenfels in this short, enthusiastic piece. Reprinted in Shrovetide in Old New Orleans, (I.26).

31   "The Writer as Seer: Ishmael Reed on Ishmael Reed." Black World 23 (June):20-34.
    Substantial, lengthy article in which Reed comments on many diverse aspects of his works and his career. Reprinted in Shrovetide in Old New Orleans, (I.26), with the title "Ishmael Reed--Self Interview."

1975

32   "The Greatest: My Own Story by Muhammad Ali." New York Times Book Review, 3 November, pp. 6, 58.
    Characterizes Ali's book as an intelligent piece of writing. It is, according to Reed, "a good old two-fisted country thumping in words; a bone-crushing, quality thriller." Reed finds some portions of the book underdeveloped, but on the whole finds it worth reading. Reprinted in Shrovetide in Old New Orleans, (I.26).

33   "Hoodoo Manifesto #2 on Criticism: The Baker-Gayle Fallacy." Black History Museum Umum Newsletter 4, no. 3-4:9-12.
    Reed takes issue with Houston Baker's review of The Last Days of Louisiana Red because Baker compares Reed's technique to that of Swift. Reed insists that his techniques take into account that satire has existed and does exist within the reader of the Afro-American literary corpus: examples abound in Guide as well as Hurston.

34   "Max Bond and Carl Anthony on Afro-American Architecture: An Interview by Ishmael Reed." Yardbird Reader. Vol. 4, pp. 12-33.
    This interview came about because Bond delivered a lecture at UC Berkeley titled "Architectural Mumbo Jumbo" in which Bond discussed a connection between Reed's Mumbo Jumbo and trends in contemporary Afro-American architecture. Bond is professor of architecture at Columbia University,

and has been commissioned for the new Martin Luther King, Jr. Center in Atlanta, Georgia. Anthony joined in the interview, as he is assistant professor of architecture at U.C. Berkeley, and is writing a book on the roots of Afro-American architecture. Anthony is also Art Commissioner of Berkeley.

35 "Native Son Lives!" Literary Calvalcade 28 (November):10, 40.
   Offers an introduction to Wright's Native Son. He sketches the short-lived history of Orson Welles's and John Houseman's dramatic adaptation of the novel. Also, Reed seeks out the contemporary parallels to life in America in the 1930s and ghetto life in America circa 1920. A brief excerpt of the play is reproduced. Reprinted in Shrovetide in Old New Orleans, (I.26).

36 "The Neo HooDoo Manifesto." In Essaying Essays: Alternative Forms of Exposition. Edited by Richard Kostelanetz. New York: Out of London Press, pp. 352-56.
   Reprint of IV.9.

37 "The Old Music." City 8 (5-18 February):no pagination.
   Discusses the changes that have taken place in black people's perceptions of the music of the South, or the "Old Country," and that until recently, the music of the South has been viewed with hostility. He notes a trend among the young black people to revive interest in this music, which is represented by such greats as Jelly Roll Morton, and "King HooDoo Zulu Louis Armstrong." Reprinted in Shrovetide in Old New Orleans, (I.26).

38 "Third World Told to Seek More Arts Money." Los Angeles Times, 29 April, Section II, p. 5.
   Adapted from an address to the Third World Writers and Thinkers Conference held during the week of April 21, 1975 in Sacramento, California. Continues his argument for financial support of the arts and formation of an Afro-American cultural bank.

1976

39 "Crushing the Mutiny." Yardbird Reader. Vol. 5, pp. 224-28.
   Reed takes considerable exception to the article by Robert Moss (1975.25) as being full of errors and racist, and notes significant comments which were made supporting Reed's point of view. He concludes that "Instead of welcoming a time in history when 'American' isn't interchangeable with rudeness, grossness and provincialism, but stands for a society where all the cultures of the world

may coexist, and in which cultural exchange thrives, they [nonwhite writers] are seen as a threat, and as even a terror. This is truly sad."

40 "Crushing the Mutiny." Melus 3, no. 2:10-12.
    Reprinted from Yardbird Reader. Vol. 5.

41 "The First Black Wasp: The Children of Ham by Claude Brown." Washington Post, 11 April, part E, pp. 1-2.
    Reed notes that his expectation of Claude Brown was to "meet Mr. Ghetto coming at me like a swaggering ostrich handing out all kind of jive, you dig? Instead I found someone who talked like the host for Masterpiece Theatre, and who ordered in French." His description of Brown provides the backdrop for the criticism leveled at Brown's book which is that it says what has already been said about heroin addiction in Harlem. Reed points out that more non-whites and suburbanites are addicted to heroin than blacks, and the liberal audience, the audience Reed identifies as the intended one for Brown's work, has turned a deaf ear-- an indifferent phony Zen Buddhist ear, possibly the new aesthetic--to the problem. The review also takes potshots at big business and the media of all forms. Reed concludes that Brown's best voice is first person and predicts that when this voice is used, post-Harlem, Brown will produce a classic. Reprinted in Shrovetide in Old New Orleans, (I.26).

42 "A Glimpse of Voodoo." Washington Post, 6 August, Section B, p. 4.
    Reed characterizes A Treasury of Afro-American Folklore by Harold Courlander, as a "worthwhile anthology that fails." He takes exception to its tone, content, and references. "No matter how diligent the author appears to have been, this is a tourists' book. . . . Cultural boasting has no place in an objective study of other peoples' cultures." Reprinted in Shrovetide in Old New Orleans, (I.26).

43 "Harlem Renaissance Day." New York Times Book Review, 29 August, p. 27.
    Reed protests criticisms by "some sullen humorless critics" of the Harlem Renaissance who have advanced the notion that "the writers weren't militant enough, that they were writing for white people. . . ." The critics' approach, says Reed, is "A literary Banana Republic approach to things by those who've forgotten that the mainstream aspiration of Afro-America is for more freedom and not slavery--including freedom of artistic expression. . . . You judge workers by the quality of their work, not by . . . whether they've successfully created a plan to

end the world's evils, or prevented the world from col-
lapsing." Reprinted in <u>Shrovetide in Old New Orleans</u>,
(I.26).

44   "Integration or Cultural Exchange?" <u>Yardbird Reader</u>.
      Vol. 5, p. 3.
          Short introductory essay to volume five of <u>Yardbird</u>
      <u>Reader</u>, in which Reed rejects the description of <u>Yardbird</u>'s
      projects as "integrationist," and asserts the "<u>Yardbird</u>
      reflects cultural exchange!"

45   "L'écrivain multi-culturel." <u>Le Monde</u> (11 June):no pagination.
          Discusses the changing American literary scene, offering
      that "No longer is American writing a country club for
      Eastern white men over 40. . . ." The balance of the arti-
      cle discusses the various artists of other cultures who are
      writing for and being published in small press publications.
      Reed believes that the large American publishing houses
      are no longer publishing poetry or fiction because it is
      unprofitable. Reed lists some of the significant writers
      who in his opinion are among the least read of the new
      writers. (Article in French.) Reprinted in <u>Shrovetide in</u>
      <u>Old New Orleans</u>, (I.26).

46   "Letters: Much Ado About Voodoo." <u>Washington Post</u>,
      5 September, Section G, p. 10.
          Reed's reply to Courlander's (1976) and Berman's (1976)
      letters about Reed's review of <u>The Treasury of Afro-</u>
      <u>American Folklore</u> ("A Glimpse of Voodoo," 1976). Reed
      defends his statements vigorously, point by point. He
      says, about midway through his letter, that Courlander's
      and Berman's attitudes seem "to be that only white scholars
      can make sense of data concerning Afro-American culture
      since those assumptions made by the people themselves are
      'unreliable,' and 'folklore,' usually meaning an unsophis-
      ticated interpretation of experience."

47   "The 'Liberal' In Us All." <u>Antaeus</u> 21/22 (Spring/Summer):
      149-54.
          Based on a speech given at the Third World Writers and
      and Thinkers Symposium, a Conference on Asian-Black-
      Chicano-Indian Writing and Thought at California State
      University, Sacramento, on April 17, 1975. Reed charac-
      terizes the Third World as divided: "We are fighting each
      other. Fighting over who's the whitest; fighting over who
      can speak English the best." He concludes, saying "We
      should proceed cautiously, scientifically, and rationally
      so that the sorry debacle which happened to the white
      liberal-black liberal doesn't happen to us." Reprinted in
      <u>Shrovetide in Old New Orleans</u>, (I.26).

48   "Pee Wee's Wreath." <u>New York Times</u>, 16 December, p. 47.
         Brief, emotional essay mourning the untimely death of
     Emmit C. Walthall, proprietor of Pee Wee's, a beloved
     hangout. "Pee Wee's was where the alienated went to have
     their community. . . . He was a black man, standing erect
     and tough, making space for himself in a world hostile to
     black men." Reprinted in <u>Shrovetide in Old New Orleans</u>,
     (I.26), with the title "The World Needs More Guys Like
     Pee Wee."

49   "<u>Remembering Josephine</u>." <u>New York Times Book Review</u>,
     12 December, pp. 5, 24.
         Reviews Stephen Papich's book, addding some anecdotes of
     his own. He finds Papich's work memorable and sensitive.
     One anecdote added was his presentation of <u>Mumbo Jumbo</u>--
     the cover having an old photo of Josephine Baker--to
     Josephine Baker in San Francisco a year before her death.

50   "You Can't Be A Literary Magazine and Hate Writers." <u>Yard-
     bird Reader</u>. Vol. 5, pp. 18-20.
         Notes the demise of <u>Black World</u> and speculates on what
     went wrong, commenting that as the editor spent more and
     more time organizing a literary event in Nigeria, "<u>Black
     World</u> came under the influence of a local Royal family
     replete with Queen Mother and Jr. Prince . . . [who] main-
     tained a literary 'enemies' list."

                              1977

51   "The Before Columbus Foundation." <u>Y'Bird Magazine</u> 1:7-8.
         Discusses the creation and operation of the Before
     Columbus Foundation, "whose aim is to begin a review of
     American history and culture in multi-cultural terms and
     to engender new multi-cultural programs."

52   "<u>Black Culture and Black Consciousness</u> by Lawrence W.
     Levine." <u>California Monthly</u> 87 (April/May):no pagination.
         Praises Levine's work on black culture as "a major work
     bound to have lasting influence." He lambasts what he
     calls the "Black Aesthetic critics" (those black univer-
     sity faculty members who insist that all writing on the
     black experience should be done by blacks and reviewed by
     them) as "a marxist front, posing the traditional problems
     for Afro-American writers." This attack is particularly
     pertinent to this review, as Reed hopes the Levine work
     will be "a new breed among white scholars of Afro-American
     culture." Reprinted in <u>American Book Review</u> 1, no. 6.

                               20

53 "A Conversation with Ralph Ellison." New York Times,
      9 July, part 17, p. 1.
          Excerpts from interview published in Y'Bird Magazine,
      1978.

54 "Hoodoo that Voodoo that You Do In New Orleans." Oui 6
      (January):124-31.
          A vivid recounting of Reed's visit to Mardi Gras, in-
      cluding considerable background regarding the holiday and
      its originators.

55 "The Multicultural Artist: A New Phase for American Litera-
      ture." San Francisco Bay Guardian 11, no. 33 (26 May):15.
          Reprint of "L'écrivain multi-culturel," Le Monde, 1976.
      (See also IV.45).

56 "Multi-Cultural Issue." Berkeley Barb, 27 May-2 June, p. 7.
          Announces the formation of the Before Columbus Founda-
      tion of which he is the chairman of the board, and points
      out the idea that an alternative distribution network needs
      to be established for non-mainstream writers. Reed re-
      iterates his refusal to demand that any writer conform to
      his aesthetic. He also questions the validity of any cul-
      tural establishment which demands aesthetic conformity from
      any artist, noting that if the small clique can dictate
      what one reads, "what other areas of life would they seek
      control over next?"

                              1978

57 "American Poetry: A Buddhist Takeover?" Black American Lit-
      erature Forum 12, no. 1, pp. 3-11.
          An interesting occasional writing reminiscent of
      nineteenth-century American authors' notebooks. It is
      organized chronologically from May 14, 1977 to October 4,
      1977 and covers Reed's experiences during his visit to
      Boulder, Colorado, and ends with his visit to Washington
      University, St. Louis. Included are discussions of
      Buddhism, an anecdote from his luncheon with Howard
      Nemerov, and a discussion of William Burroughs's work The
      Job.

58 "The Essential Ellison." (With Quincy Troupe and Steve
      Cannon.) Y'Bird Magazine 1, no. 1:130-59.
          Ellison is questioned and discusses at length a great
      variety of topics, including the differences between the
      writers of the 40s and 50s and those who emerged during the
      60s and 70s; Jewish intellectuals and their criticism of
      Afro-American writers; the American Academy of Arts and

Letters; Ellison's relationships with Richard Wright and
Chester Himes; and Ellison's career and his opinions about
the state of Afro-American literature.

59   "From the Final Appeal." CoEvolution Quarterly 19 (Fall):
     63-67.
          Takes up a variety of subjects in an additive fashion.
     His concerns range from the media to multinational con-
     glomerates. He spends a good deal of time analyzing the
     national scene from a non-white position, overlaying and
     juxtaposing various "facts." He concludes that "at this
     time in American history we are like spirits talking gib-
     berish through different dimensions and stupid men do not
     make good mediums."

60   "An Interview with Rudolfo Anaya." San Francisco Review of
     Books 4, no. 2 (June):9-12, 34.
          Interviewing Rudolfo Anaya, a Southwest Chicano writer,
     Reed leads the discussion to six prominent Southwest
     writers and their works. The interview touches on such
     subjects as violence and its roots in the Southwest, trends
     in Chicano writing, and the philosophy of Anaya.

61   "Ishmael Reed Interviews Ralph Ellison." In Before Columbus
     Foundation Catalog One: Contemporary American Literature.
     Edited by Robert Callahan and David Meltzer. Berkeley,
     Calif.: Before Columbus Foundation, pp. 53-54.
          Excerpts from "The Essential Ellison," Y'Bird Magazine,
     1978.

62   Preface to Yardbird Lives! Edited by Ishmael Reed and Al
     Young. New York: Grove Press, pp. 13-15.
          Short introduction of Yardbird Lives!, briefly describ-
     ing its origins in the Yardbird Readers. Characterizes
     19 Necromancers From Now as having "proved that Afro-
     American writers differed when times were demanding
     uniformity among them."

63   "St. Louis Woman." New Letters 45:33-36.
          A zany local color piece about St. Louis, W. C. Handy,
     and St. Louis women.

                              1979

64   "All-Night Visitors: A Review." Black American Literature
     Forum 13, no. 2 (Summer):73.
          Review of Clarence Major's first novel, which has not
     been made public until now.

65   "Excerpts from Ishmael Reed's Address at Guild Annual Meet-
        ing." Authors Guild Bulletin (April–May):5–6.
            Quotes from a speech Reed delivered about a new multi-
        cultural destiny for American writing.

66   "Is The Only Cultural Advantage To California That You Can
        Make A Right Turn On A Red Light?" In Calafia: The
        California Poetry. Edited by Ishmael Reed. Berkeley,
        Calif.: Y'Bird Books, pp. xxxv–xliii.
            Points up the rich multi-cultural origins and develop-
        ment of the state of Calfiornia, and then states that the
        volume "attempts to bring together the poetry of different
        California cultures under one roof." In concluding, he
        says "If . . . California is the United States' window on
        the future, then the prospect for a diverse, national
        poetry, instead of the various sects of the moment, are
        good."

67   "Tale of Two Cities: Zebra." New West 4, no. 24 (19 Novem-
        ber):137–38.
            Criticizes author Clark Howard for his lurid portrayal
        of the Zebra killers in Howard's book. Reed is particu-
        larly distressed with the orientation of the book, which
        describes the childishness of the Black Muslim killers.
        Reed wonders how Howard was able to gather some of the
        details supplied: "'I wondered how Howard knew the size of
        the genitals a killer exercised during a rape scene." Or
        "'He went inside and found the candy section. Much as a
        child would do . . . .' There is no way of Howard knowing
        this; he made it up." Reed also takes the opportunity to
        discuss racism in America, and takes note that during the
        Zebra killings in San Francisco, the entire black community
        was under suspicion by the Bay Area police. Reed acknowl-
        edges that "It won't be the first or last time in American
        history when an entire community came under suspicion be-
        cause of the crimes of a few."

1980

68   "The American Literary Scene As a White Settler's Fortress."
        In The Art of Literary Publishing: Editors on Their Craft.
        Edited by Bill Henderson. Yonkers, N.Y.: Pushcart Press,
        pp. 100–105.
            Reed discusses the various publications which he has
        edited including Yardbird Reader. As well he discusses
        the impact of monocultural press on both the American lit-
        erary experience and the international literary experience.
        Reed decries the monoculturalists represented on the
        various funding agencies for the arts and on the various
        grant-funding organizations. Finally, Reed snipes at the

literary experiences presented to students in most American universities and then relates his experiences as a teacher at Berkeley who put together a literary publication of the students' writing known as <u>Will It Fly</u>.

69   "Hell Hath No Fury." (A drama) Unpublished.
       Play first presented by The Playwrights and Directors Project of The Actors Studio as part of their Works in Process 1980 program, on Sunday, June 1, 1980, in New York. The play was directed by Jason Buzas. (Information from playbill; no plot details available.)

70   "How Not to Get The Infidel to Talk The King's Talk." In <u>The State of the Language</u>. Edited by Leonard Michaels and Christopher Ricks. Berkeley: University of California Press, pp. 180-81.
       Reed raises the problem of the uses of Black English, rising to its challengers like Dick Cavett and John Simon. Aptly, Reed points to the obvious uses of language as often situation-centered. Likewise he points out that those raised on Elvis Presley, both black and white, might very well speak Black English. Summing, Reed notes that to teach "standard English" to Black English speakers based on the assumption that "Standard English" will help one get ahead ". . . will be seen through by the millions of Black English followers both overt and covert."

71   "Ishmael Reed." <u>Focus Magazine</u> (KOED TV) (March):35-36.
       Reed gives a fast but thorough detailing of his publishing activities to date, and talks briefly about how living on the West Coast has affected his life.

1981

72   "Black Macho, White Macho: The Stale Drama." <u>Playgirl</u> (March):12-13, 110.
       (Examined in galley proof.) Reed takes up the argument of black male sexual prowess and points out that the "myth" of black males is overblown. He also says that the white male also has a macho complex; both groups have attitudes harmful to themselves. In sum, he finds that blacks have been denied their ultimate machoness because, he postulates if America enters a nuclear war the finger activating the nuclear machine will probably be white.

73   "Ismael Reed Replies to Amiri Baraka." Unpublished.
       (Article examined in manuscript.) Multifaceted interview with Reed in which he discussed Baraka's charges that

he (Reed) is a conservative. Reed also advances his
opinions and facts concerning a number of other points of
controversy he has had with Baraka.

V POETRY

Poems Appearing in Anthologies

1964

1   LOWENFELS, WALTER, ed. Poets of Today: A New American
       Anthology. New York: International Publishing Co.
          Includes: "Ghost in Birmingham," pp. 109-11.

1967

2   LOWENFELS, WALTER, ed. Where is Vietnam? American Poets
       Respond: An Anthology of Contemporary Poems. Garden
       City, N.Y.: Doubleday & Company.
          Includes: "Gangster's death," p. 107.

1969

3   LOWENFELS, WALTER, ed. In A Time of Revolution: Poems From
       Out Third World. New York: Random House.
          Includes: "Jackal Headed Cowboy," pp. 114-16.

4   MAJOR, CLARENCE, ed. The New Black Poetry. New York:
       International Publishers.
          Includes: "I Am a Cowboy in the Boat of Ra," pp. 109-11.

1970

5   EASTMAN, ARTHUR M. et al., eds. The Norton Anthology of
       Poetry. New York: W. W. Norton & Co.
          Includes: "beware: do not read this poem," p. 1189;
       "I am a Cowboy in the Boat of Ra," p. 1188.

6   HUGHES, LANGSTON, and BONTEMPS, ARNA, eds. The Poetry of The
       Negro 1746-1970. Garden City, N.Y.: Doubleday & Co.
          Includes: "feral pioneers," p. 415.

7   JORDAN, JUNE, ed. <u>Soulscript: Afro-American Poetry</u>.
      Garden City, N.Y.: Doubleday & Co.
         Includes: "beware: do not read this poem," pp. 64-65;
      "off d pig," pp. 90-91.

8   MILLER, ADAM DAVID, ed. <u>Dices or Black Bones: Black Voices
      of the Seventies</u>. Boston: Houghton Mifflin Co.
         Includes: "I am a Cowboy in the Boat of Ra," pp. 129-30;
      "badman of the guest professor," pp. 131-34; "beware: do
      not read this poem," pp. 135-36.

1971

9   FORD, NICK AARON, ed. <u>Black Insights: Significant Literature
      by Black Americans--1760 to the Present</u>. Waltham, Mass.:
      Ginn & Co.
         Includes: "I am a Cowboy in the Boat of Ra," p. 310.

10   HARVEY, NICK, ed. <u>Mark in Time: Portraits and Poetry/San
      Francisco</u>. San Francisco: Glide Publications.
         Includes: "Al Capone in Alaska," p. 74.

11   HAYDEN, ROBERT et al., eds. <u>Afro-American Literature: An
      Introduction</u>. New York: Harcourt Brace Jovanovich.
         Includes: "I am a Cowboy in the Boat of Ra," pp. 151-52.

12   LOWENFELS, WALTER, ed. <u>The Writing on The Wall: 108 American
      Poems of Protest</u>. Garden City, N.Y.: Doubleday.
         Includes: "Sermonette," p. 12.

13   MURRAY, ALMA, and THOMAS, ROBERT, eds. <u>Major Black Writers</u>.
      New York: <u>Scholastic Book Services</u>.
         Includes: "beware: do not read this poem," pp. 200-201.

14   RANDALL, DUDLEY, ed. <u>The Black Poets</u>. New York: Bantam
      Books.
         Includes: "badman of the guest professor," p. 284;
      "Black Power Poem," p. 288; "beware: do not read this
      poem," p. 288.

1972

15   ADOFF, ARNOLD, ed. <u>The Poetry of Black America: Anthology of
      the 20th Century</u>. New York: Harper & Row.
         Includes: "Rain rain on the splintered girl," p. 327;
      "Sermonette," p. 328; "beware: do not read this poem,"
      p. 328; "I am a Cowboy in the Boat of Ra," p. 330;
      "Gangster's death," p. 331; "feral Pioneers," p. 335;
      "Instructions to a princess," p. 336.

16   BARNES, RICHARD G., comp. <u>Episodes in Five Poetic Traditions</u>.
      San Francisco: Chandler Publishing Co.
          Includes: "I am a Cowboy in the Boat of Ra,"
      pp. 463-64; "beware: do not read this poem," pp. 465-66.

17   CHAPMAN, ABRAHAM, ed. <u>New Black Voices: An Anthology of</u>
      <u>Contemporary Afro-American Literature</u>. New York: New
      American Library.
          Includes: "catechism of d neoamerican hoodoo church,"
      pp. 329-34.

18   KOSTELANETZ, RICHARD, ed. <u>Seeing through Shuck</u>. New York:
      Ballantine Books.
          Includes: "catechism of d neoamerican hoodoo church,"
      pp. 80-86.

1973

19   BREMAN, PAUL, ed. <u>You Better Believe It</u>. New York: Penguin.
          Includes: "catechism of d neoamerican hoodoo church,"
      pp. 401-2.

20   QUASHA, GEORGE, and ROTHENBERG, JEROME, eds. <u>America A</u>
      <u>Prophecy: A New Reading of American Poetry From Pre-</u>
      <u>Columbian Times to the Present</u>. New York: Random House.
          Includes: "I am a Cowboy in the Boat of Ra," p. 293.

1974

21   HILL, HELEN, and PERKINS, AGNES, comps. <u>New Coasts and</u>
      <u>Strange Harbors: Discovering Poems</u>. New York: Thomas Y.
      Crowell Co.
          Includes: "beware: do not read this poem," pp. 251-52.

22   KENNEDY, X. J., ed. <u>An Introduction to Poetry</u>. Boston:
      Little, Brown & Co. 3rd ed.
          Includes: ".05," p. 98; "I am a Cowboy in the Boat of
      Ra," pp. 235-36.

23   NIMS, JOHN F., ed. <u>Western Wind: An Introduction to Poetry</u>.
      New York: Random House.
          Includes: "beware: do not read this poem," p. 249.

1975

24   LOWENFELS, WALTER, ed. <u>For Neruda, For Chile</u>. Boston:
      Beacon Press.

27

Includes: "Poem delivered before Assembly of Colored People held at Glide Memorial Church, October 4, 1973 and Called to Protest Recent Events in the Sovereign Republic of Chile," pp. 156-58.

25 MIRIKITANI, JANICE et al., eds. <u>Time to Greez: Incantations from the Third World</u>. San Francisco: Glide Publications/ Third World Communications.
Includes: "Sky Diving," pp. 121-22.

26 TROUPE, QUINCY, ed. <u>Giant Talk: An Anthology of Third World Writings</u>. New York: Random House.
Includes: "Dragon's Blood," p. 331; "dress rehearsal paranoia #2," p. 332; "I am a Cowboy in the Boat of Ra," pp. 279-81; "White Hope," p. 331.

1976

27 HEYEN, WILLIAM, ed. <u>American Poets in 1976</u>. Indianapolis, Ind.: Bobbs Merrill Co.
Includes: "Sputin," pp. 267-68; "The Reactionary Poet," pp. 270-72; "Flight to Canada," pp. 272-74.

28 WAGNER, LINDA W., and MEAD, C. DAVID, eds. <u>Introducing Poems</u>. New York: Harper & Row.
Includes: "beware: do not read this poem," pp. 302-3.

1977

29 ADOFF, ARNOLD, ed. <u>Celebrations: A New Anthology of Black Poetry</u>. Chicago: Follett Publishing Co.
Includes: "Untitled I," p. 95; "Instructions to a Princess," p. 114; "beware: do not read this poem," pp. 134-35; "The Reactionary Poet," pp. 135-37.

1978

30 CALLAHAN, ROBERT et al., eds. <u>Before Columbus Foundation Catalog One: Contemporary American Literature 1978-1979</u>. Berkeley, Calif.: Before Columbus Foundation.
Includes: "Pocadonia," p. 102.

1979

31 REED, ISHMAEL, ed. <u>Calafia: The California Poetry</u>. Berkeley, Calif.: Y'Bird Books.

Includes: "Jacket Notes," pp. 278-79; "The Author Reflects on His 35th Birthday," pp. 279-80; "Foolology," pp. 282-83; "Untitled," p. 283.

Poems Published Separately

1963

32 "The Ghost in Birmingham." Liberator 3 (November):21.

33 "Patrice." Umbra 2 (December):36.

34 "Time and the Eagle." Umbra 2 (December):5-6.

1966

35 "Rain rain on the splintered Girl." Negro Digest 15 (September):68-69.

1968

36 "I am a Cowboy in the Boat of Ra." Noose 1 (June): no pagination.

37 "Sermonette: poem." Negro Digest 17 (August):53.

38 "for cardinal spellman who hated voo doo." I-KON 1, no. 5 (March 27):32.

1969

39 "Badman of the Guest Professor." Negro Digest 19 (November): 44-47.
    Later revised for inclusion in Conjure. (Note: This poem also appeared in part in Negro Digest 18 (September): 17; but only a portion of the first page of the poem was printed and it cuts off in midsentence.)

40 "The Feral Pioneers." For Now 10 (1969):1-2.

1970

41 "Hoodoo Artist vs. DeGaulle: poem." Black World 19 (September):33.

42   "Paul Lawrence Dunbar in the Tenderloin." Essence 1
      (October):6.

43   "Why I often Allude to Osiris." Essence 1 (October):6.

1971

44   "Aide Denies LBJ Called Pope 'A Dumb Cunt'." Cricket: Black
      Music in Evolution 4 (December):65.

45   "beware: do not read this poem." Scholastic Scope 15, no. 11
      (6 December):6.

1972

46   "Haitians." Yardbird Reader. Vol. 1, pp. 162-163.

47   "Kali's Galaxy." Works 3 (Winter):23.

48   "Kali's Galaxy." Yardbird Reader. Vol. 1, pp. 163-164.

49   "The Kardek Method." Yardbird Reader. Vol. 1, pp. 161-162.

50   "Monsters fragment." Friends Seminary Review (May):46.

51   "Poison Light." Works 3 (Winter):22.

52   "Poison Light." Yardbird Reader. Vol. 1, pp. 164-165.

53   "Railroad Bill, A Conjure Man." Yardbird Reader. Vol. 1,
      pp. 155-161.

54   "Skirt Dance." Yardbird Reader. Vol. 1, p. 163.

1973

55   "Antigone, This Is It." Black World 22 (September):67-68.

56   "Back to Africa." Saturday Review/World 1 (23 October):61.

57   "The Lost State of Franklin." Friends Seminary Review, p. 15.

1974

58   "Sky Diving." Hambone [Stanford University] (August), no
      pagination.

1975

59   "Return of Julian the Apostate to Rome." Iowa Review 6
        (Spring):6.

60   "Sky Diving." San Francisco Chronicle: California Living
        Magazine, 25 May, no pagination.

1976

61   "From the Files of Agent 22." Yardbird Reader. Vol. 5,
        p. 315.

62   "Poetry Makes Rhythm in Philosophy." Buffalo: Friends of the
        Lockwood Memorial Library, State University of New York,
        Christmas Broadside no. 9. 31 cm.

1977

63   ".05." KPFA Folio (May):6-7.

64   "Rough Trade Slumlord Totem." Black Scholar 8 (March):27.

65   "The Saga of Third World Belle." American Poetry Review 6,
        no. 1 (January/February):26.

66   "Sixth Street Corporate War." San Francisco Bay Guardian 11,
        no. 22 (10 March):10.

67   "Skydiving." In "Poets on Poetry," by Herb Kohl. Teacher 94
        (April):50. (See also 1977.19.)

68   "Soul Proprietorship." New World Journal (Spring):83-84.

1978

69   "Soul Proprietorship." In "Ishmael Reed," by Gerald Duff
        (1978.11, pp. 420-21).
          (Note: Duff indicates this is the typescript of a
        previously unpublished poem.)

70   "The Sparrow Decision." Black Scholar 10, nos. 3 & 4 (November/
        December):23.

Undated

70a "Untitled." San Francisco Bay Guardian, 5 October, p. 13.

Writings by Ishmael Reed

1980

71 "Judas." <u>Poets and Writers, Inc.: Tenth Birthday Party</u>.
    Roseland, N.Y., 22 October, p. 34.

1981

72 "Petite Kid Everett." <u>The Buffalo News</u>, 4 January, no
    pagination.

VI MEDIA

Sound Recordings

1 <u>The East Village Other</u> ESP S-1032 (phonodisc).

2 <u>Ishmael Reed and Michael Harper Reading in the UCSD
   (University of California, San Diego) New Poetry Series</u>.
   Winter 1977 (7" Reel Tape).

3 <u>Ishmael Reed Reading His Poetry</u>. Recorded at The Temple of
   Zeus, Cornell University, April 23, 1976. 65 min.
   (Cassette).

4 <u>New Jazz Poets</u> AR Records BR 461 Broadside (phonodisc).

5 <u>The Steve Cannon Show: A Quarterly Audio-Cassette Radio Show
   Magazine</u>. Vol. 1. New York: Reed, Cannon & Johnson Com-
   munications.
       Side two: A dramatic episode from <u>The Last Days of
   Louisiana Red</u>, starring Al Young as the Liberal, Ray
   Johnson as Kingfish, and Victor Cruz as Street (Cassette).

Video Tapes

6 <u>1st World Symposium</u>. Central Washington State College,
   50 minute B/W edited standard ATV tape. No date.

7 <u>Personal Problems</u>. Executive Producer of a pilot episode of a
   soap opera.

8 <u>San Francisco Poetry Center Videotape Library</u>. San Francisco
   State University. 1973-1974.

9 <u>Writers Forum</u>. Writers Forum, Department of English, State
   University, College at Brockport, Brooklyn, New York. No
   date.

Writings by Ishmael Reed

Multi-Media

10　The Lost State of Franklin.　Reed collaborated with Carla
　　　　Blank and Suzushi Hanayagi on a multi-media mystery.　1976.

PART TWO

Writings about Ishmael Reed

1967

1   ANON. "The Free-Lance Pallbearers by Ishmael Reed." Fort
     Worth (Tex.) Star, 12 November, no pagination.
          Brief notice of the novel. "The book stands as a sort
     of study in language--hippie-talk with a savage bite."

2   ANON. "The Free-Lance Pallbearers." Kirkus Reviews
     (15 September):1163.
          An abrupt dismissal of the work: "this is diarrhea of
     the typewriter. We can recommend the same treatment:
     FLUSH! HAR HAR HAR!"

3   ANON. "The Free-Lance Pallbearers." Pittsburgh Press,
     22 October, no pagination.
          Abbreviated notice. "Not easy reading, but it is strong
     and imaginative, with real shock value and a dazzling play
     on words."

4   ANON. "The Free-Lance Pallbearers." Publishers' Weekly 192
     (11 September):66.
          Includes an abbreviated plot summary and concludes that
     "This bitter, caustic, bawdy novel rips the American estab-
     lishment to pieces. Not easy reading by any means, it is
     strong and imaginative, with a real shock value and a daz-
     zling play on words."

5   GREENYA, JOHN. "A Novel of Satire But It's Overdone."
     Washington Star, 5 November, no pagination.
          Discusses Free-Lance Pallbearers but finds that "this
     book is bad for a large number of reasons. . . . The way
     he presents his case is so strange that the book's message
     gets lost very early. The result is a very self-indulgent
     piece of prose that reads as if the author didn't care
     whether anybody could like or understand it. Perhaps
     that's the point, but what a shame."

1967

6   HOGAN, WILLIAM. "New Novelists and Old Problems." <u>San Francisco Chronicle</u>, 29 November, no pagination.
        Includes mention of a number of "first novels." <u>Free-Lance Pallbearers</u> "is a feverish little opus, a madly exuberant fantasy." The volume is "an almost successful slapstick comedy that loses its sting simply because the joke goes on too long."

7   KATZMAN, ALLAN. "Books." <u>East Village Other</u>, 16 July, p. 14.
        Reviews <u>Yellow Back Radio Broke-Down</u> which is found to be a "scatalogical showdown." Reed's use of language is such that "one ends up with ropeburns trying to hold onto his prose." Katzman concludes that "the novel is not dead when the reins are held by a top dog who has complete command of his craft and its language."

8   _____. "Books." <u>East Village Other</u> 2, no. 23 (15 October/ 1 November):17, 20, 23.
        A prepublication review of Reed's first novel, <u>Free-Lance Pallbearers</u>. Notes that the <u>East Village Other</u>'s own rock group "The Fugs" is attacked in the book. Included is a very long plot summary.

9   KINNAMON, KENETH. "<u>The Free-Lance Pallbearers</u>." <u>Negro American Literature Forum</u> 1 (Winter):18.
        Contends that Reed's first novel has a problem in that it aims at too many targets. "Mr. Reed's basic difficulty is simple enough. His scatter gun technique disperses rather than concentrates his satiric energy." Kinnamon states his belief that "the most pervasive unifying device is the central metaphor of shit, of which the novel is full." He asserts that "Bukka and his playmates owe a great deal to Burroughs, Barth, Heller, Southern, and the rest, but perhaps they owe even more to the wisecrack-and-slapstick satire of <u>Mad</u> magazine." Kinnamon concludes by saying that Reed has a great deal of talent for satire and "It is to be hoped that he utilizes [it] to better advantage in his second novel than he has in his first."

10   LESHKOL, ABRAHAM. "<u>The East Village Other</u>: 'All the News That's Hip to Print.'" <u>Fact</u> 4 (May-June):42-43.
        A general article concerning the <u>East Village Other</u>; it contains a history of the newspaper and shows Ishmael Reed's influence and role in its founding.

1968

11   MAYER, DUANE. "Serious Novel or Nonsense?" (Oklahoma City)
      Oklahoman, 5 November, no pagination.
          Depicts The Free-Lance Pallbearers as nonsense. "Most
      of the time, . . . Ishmael Reed makes poor music--perhaps
      just practicing--putting down screeches and grunts."

                              1968

1   ADLER, DICK. "Not in the Boy Scout Manual." Book World
      (3 March):20.
          Finds Free-Lance Pallbearers "as 'stantial a novel as
      you're likely to bite into all year." Adler also finds
      Reed's prowess as a novelist "much in evidence in this
      thin, though very funny book [so] that Baden-Powell's loss
      is our gain."

2   BLACKBURN, SARA. "Book Marks." Nation 206 (5 February):186.
          Indicates that the plot is thin to invisible but con-
      cludes by saying "The Free-Lance Pallbearers succeeds in
      doing in 155 pages what Norman Mailer's Why Are We In
      Vietnam? swiped valiantly at. If comparisons are made they
      should be to Burroughs but this novel is Mr. Reed's own."

3   FETLER, ANDREW. "Three First Novels: Contrasts." Boston
      Globe, 25 January, no pagination.
          Characterizes Free-Lance Pallbearers as "another piece
      of self-indulgence . . . [a] text for a runaway comic
      book."

4   JOYE, BARBARA. "Literature of Race and Culture: Satire and
      Alienation in Soulville." Phylon 29, no. 4:410-12.
          Asserts in this discussion of Free-Lance Pallbearers
      that "for the moment, we have only a disorganized collec-
      tion of excellent ideas and brilliant but isolated
      vignettes." Excerpt reprinted in 1980.4.

5   KIMBALL, GEORGE. "Books: The Free-Lance Pallbearers."
      Escapade 13 (July):45.
          Kimball points up the fact that Free-Lance Pallbearers
      has been ignored by most major reviewers and consigned to
      the ranks of "The Underground Press." He finds that if
      Reed weren't black the novel would probably be offensive.
      On the other hand, Kimball praises Reed for refusing to
      "stay in line" to appease the literary establishment. In
      sum, Kimball finds "Reed hasn't railed out against Whitey
      by name, but neither has he compromised himself in order

1968

to accommodate Whitey's reviewers, and those honky critics
have repaid him in kind."

6 LIPTON, LAWRENCE. "Robin the Cock and Doopeyduk Doing the
   Boogaloo In Harry Sam With Rusty Jethroe and Letterhead
   America." Cavalier 18 (April):70-74.
       Lipton examines some of the historical predecessors of
   Reed--the Beat writers of the fifties. Lipton classifies
   Reed with the Hip Sixties movement in his examination of
   Free-Lance Pallbearers. Comparing Reed and Mailer, the
   reviewer finds it significant that they "have both been
   connected in one way or another with the underground
   press."

7 PERKINS, MICHAEL. "Books: The Free-Lance Pallbearers."
   Village Voice (28 March):7.
       Finds the novel to be "a good first novel: its major
   fault is simply that it has come along at the wrong time."
   Nevertheless, Perkins does find the language in the novel
   rewarding: "It is frenetic, supercharged, . . . desperate."

8 SHEPARD, WALT. "When State Magicians Fail: An Interview with
   Ishmael Reed." Nickel Review (28 August-10 September):
   72-75.
       In this interview after the publication of Free-Lance
   Pallbearers, Reed indicates his animosity toward James
   Baldwin, describing Baldwin's works as "those Jewish books
   by James Baldwin." Reed also indicates that he was one of
   the founders of the East Village Other. Concerning Pallbearers, Reed says "I think it's a comic book; that's what
   I was trying to get into."

9 SWORDS, BETT. "Three Books Present Diversity of Humor."
   Denver Post, 21 January, no pagination.
       Includes brief comment on The Free-Lance Pallbearers.
   "The book is a prime example of black humor, where any
   laughter is bound to be uncomfortable: the comedy of the
   gruesome. Black humor does not refer to race, but to a
   type of humor suited to basic issues--a last refuge of
   indignation."

10 TUCKER, MARTIN. "The Free-Lance Pallbearers." Commonweal 87
   (28 January):508.
       Cautiously finds Reed's novel an interesting attempt at
   the grotesque for a laugh and, further, that Reed "relies
   on the in-joke too much. This array is losing some of its
   power of surprise." Excerpt reprinted in 1980.4.

11 W, R. "The Free-Lance Pallbearers by Ishmael Reed." New
     Haven (Conn.) Register, 10 March, no pagination.
          Asserts that this is an "unamusing comic novel." "More
     micturition than fiction, displaying more of proctology
     than psychology, the novel is by an inventive young man who
     avoids the trite but fails either to amuse or enlighten."

1969

1 ABBOTT, STEVE. "Beyond the Signs." Great Speckled Bird
     (1 December):15.
          Reed is said to be following the mainstream of Afro-
     American literature in that "his protagonists are displaced
     but rightfully rebellious in their search for identity."
     Abbott says that Free-Lance Pallbearers falls short and
     lacks structure. "The novel's humor often becomes merely
     gimmicky." But Yellow Back Radio Broke-Down "goes far in
     correcting the weaknesses. . . . Reed's improved style is
     directly relatable to the tighter structure of his alle-
     gory." Abbott concludes that Yellow Back is "the best
     allegorical novel since Ken Kesey's One Flew Over the
     Cuckoo's Nest and Ishmael Reed . . . deserves to be better
     known. Dig it! This cat knows the signs."

2 ADLER, DICK. "Fiba: Book Review." Fiba: Actualité
     (Spring):55.
          Substantially the same review of Free-Lance Pallbearers
     as 1968.1.

3 ANON. "News About Books." (Highpoint, N.C.) Enterprise,
     24 August, no pagination.
          Brief overview of Reed's career to date.

4 No entry.

5 ANON. "1985." Times Literary Supplement, 9 January, p. 31.
          Points to Free-Lance Pallbearers as "impossibly bizarre
     and wholly directionless. . . . the novel progresses--a
     series of wild erratically linked hallucinations whose
     cumulative effect is unsettling and decidedly exhausting."

6 ANON. "Parody Takes Look at American Dilemma." Columbia
     Missourian, 14 December, no pagination.
          In this very short review of Yellow Back Radio Broke-
     Down, the reviewer claims it "takes a hilariously uninhib-
     ited look at American history, the American dilemma and
     what has become of the American dream."

1969

7 ANON. "Reed, Ishmael. "Yellow Back Radio Broke-Down."
   Kirkus Reviews 37 (1 June):611.
      A brief notice characterizes the work as "a stoned
   fantasy written on high glee and black hipster credos."
   The reviewer finds Reed to be "raw, rollicking, irrev-
   erent, . . . a preachy Chester Himes and just as cheeky."

8 BREMAN, PAUL. "Poetry into the 'Sixties." In The Black
   American Writer. Edited by C. W. E. Bigsby. Vol. 2.
   Deland, Fla.: Everett Edwards, p. 101.
      Reed is mentioned, called "probably the best black poet
   writing today "

9 CADE, TONI. "The Free-Lance Pallbearers." Liberator 9
   (June):20.
      Cade compares the novel to the writings of Orwell,
   Vonnegut, Burgess, and Bradbury. She finds the strength
   of the novel to be its length, so that the "fresh and
   arresting diction never becomes tiresome. the gaming with
   names and types never becomes strained." The review en-
   courages further reading of Reed.

10 CHILDS, JAMES. "Yellow Back Radio Broke-Down." Library
   Journal 94 (July):2643.
      A brief review that compares the novel to Patchen's
   Journal of Albion Moonlight, published in 1961. The
   reviewer also points out that the Loop Garoo Kid is not the
   "Negro Cowboy killed by John Wesley Hardin; rather he is
   the Negro Cowboy who kills Hardin."

11 CRABBE, KEN. "Previewing Books." (Augusta, Ga.) Sunday
   Chronicle-Herald, 3 August, p. 68.
      Yellow Back Radio Broke-Down is "a wicked parody of the
   Wild Old West that has got to be what an old maiden great
   aunt was wont to call 'a caution.'"

12 DARLING, LYNN. "Yellow Back Radio Broke-Down." Harvard
   Crimson, 2 December, no pagination.
      "It's a roughshod book, and it probably won't get to you
   much unless the back of your mind happens to resemble
   Reed's."

13 FAIR, RONALD L. "A Fiction Masterpiece." Press (Birmingham,
   N.Y.), 17 August, no pagination.
      Reprint of 1969.19.

14   _____. "'Hoodoo' Western Provides Prime Spot for Fresh
        Satire." <u>News</u> (Birmingham, Ala.), 10 August, no pagina-
        tion.
            Reprint of 1969.19.

15   _____. "Masterpiece of Laughter." <u>San Francisco Examiner</u>,
        18 August, no pagination.
            Reprint of 1969.19.

16   _____. "Myth-Making in Fine Spoof." <u>World Herald</u> (Omaha,
        Neb.), 10 August, p. 31.
            Reprint of 1969.19.

17   _____. "This Masterpiece is Funny." <u>News American</u> (Baltimore,
        Md.), 5 August, no pagination.
            Reprint of 1969.19.

18   _____. "Welcome Burst of Satire From a New 'Old West.'"
        <u>Evening News</u> (Buffalo, N.Y.), 16 August, no pagination.
            Reprint of 1969.19.

19   _____. "You'll Laugh and Learn a Lot." <u>Chicago Sun Times</u>,
        3 August, no pagination.
            Asserts that in <u>Yellow Back Radio Broke-Down</u>, all the
        time Reed is "making us laugh, he is also enlightening and
        educating us about the business of making myths, and in-
        forming us about what life in our time is <u>really</u> like.
        Reed is not only a major new talent, he is a colossal one."

20   FIESS, MARY. "Today: Black Writers Offer Diversity."
        <u>Caellian</u>, 7 November, p. 3.
            Reports appearance by Reed and Addison Gayle. "Reed
        concentrated on the current scene and the diversity mani-
        fest by black artists today."

21   FIOFORI, TAM. "<u>Yellow Back Radio Broke-Down</u>." <u>Negro Digest</u>
        (December):95-97.
            Fiofori does not find Reed's style like Burroughs's (an
        idea proffered) but rather finds it similar to Natural
        "Fictionist" Amos Tutuola's <u>Night in the Forest</u> and Miguel
        Asturias's <u>Mulata</u>. Fiofori suggests that "Ishmael Reed
        got his 'Mojo' working here and it will work on you if you
        see, feel the show, and don't stop to think about how."

1969

22 FLEISCHER, LEONORE. "Black Magic Under the Blue Skies."
    Chicago Tribune Book World, 10 August, p. 3.
        Asserts that beneath the facade of humor in Yellow Back
    Radio Broke-Down is an "intensely disciplined, intensely
    allegorical work of art." Fleischer also points out that
    the title of the work is "exactly half of a dactylic
    hexameter, the meter used by Homer." Further, "Reed tells
    us that all gods of reason are dead, but he finds an art-
    ist's solace in the dark and manic gods of long ago."
    There is some interesting Egyptian religious history re-
    counted in the short review, as well as an explanation of
    the word "loup-garou" which is French for werewolf, an
    occult word in Haiti and Africa.

23 GONCALVES, JOE. "An Afterword" [to "When State Magicians
    Fail"] (see 1968.4). Journal of Black Poetry 1 (Summer-
    Fall):75-77.
        Goncalves has launched a vitriolic attack on Reed:
    "Meanwhile Reed, drunk, sniffing white girls, dependent,
    lays dead about the white man's fort. --Or maybe 'lays
    dead' is too strong--he is still a 'critic' and though that
    may not be enough, it is at least a start."

24 GORDON, ANDREW. "Black Magic." (Berkeley) Daily Californian,
    4 November, no pagination.
        Yellow Back Radio Broke-Down and Free-Lance Pallbearers
    are discussed. "Reed . . . has developed a wacky style
    wholly unto himself, which swings with the poetry of slang,
    bop talk, and a solo scat singer traversing forty-seven
    miles of barbed wire with a cobra snake for a necktie.
    . . . Ishmael Reed wages literary guerilla warfare, posing
    a counter absurdity which fights dirty against the insanity
    of America today."

25 GREENE, DANIEL St. ALBIN. "'Horse Opera' is Staged in Pop-Art
    Burlesque." National Observer, 25 August, p. 17.
        Views Reed as "an independent cuss" who "never gets hung
    up on character development, historical integrity, and con-
    sistency of setting . . ." to the extent that "the reader
    often wonders where the author has taken him." Yellow Back
    Radio Broke-Down is viewed as "an ingenious and incisive
    work of satire."

26 GREENE, DANIEL [St. ALBIN]. "In Prose and Poetry: The New
    Black Voices." National Observer, 14 July, p. 18.
        Surveys several young emerging black writers: among
    them Nathan Heard, Lennox Raphael, Don L. Lee, Larry Neal,
    Julius Lester, Ishmael Reed. "One of the most caustic

1969

critics of the restrictive 'black consciousness' school is Ishmael Reed." The article makes brief comment on Reed's activities and ideology, and characterizes Free-Lance Pallbearers as a "hilarious outrageous satire."

26a GROSS, ROBERT. "Black Novelists: Our Turn." Newsweek 73 (16 June):96.
       Short notice of both Free-Lance Pallbearers and Yellow Back Radio Broke-Down which appears as part of an article on several black novelists.

27 HILDICK, WALLACE. "Young Writers." The Listener 81 (9 January):56.
       Points out that Reed needs to re-establish the "old orthodox cunning art of timing." In addition to Free-Lance Pallbearers, the article also discusses An Abdication by J. S. Mitchell and Run Come See Jerusalem by David Coxhead.

28 HOWE, IRVING. "New Black Writers." Harper's Magazine 239 (December):130-31, 133, 135, 137, 141.
       The section on Reed in this article, which includes many other black writers, is a short dismissal. Free-Lance Pallbearers is panned: "Packed with Mad Magazine silliness though his work is, Mr. Reed has one saving virtue: he is hopelessly good natured. . . . He may intend his books as a black variation of Jonathan Swift; they emerge closer to the commercial cooings of Captain Kangaroo." Yellow Back Radio Broke-Down is also mentioned. Excerpts reprinted in 1978.48 and 1980.4.

29 KATZMAN, ALLAN. "Books." East Village Other 4, no. 33 (16 July):14.
       Notes that Reed has revitalized the form of the novel with Yellow Back Radio Broke-Down.

30 LEHMANN-HAUPT, CHRISTOPHER. "Will the Real 'Black Esthetic' Please Stand Up?" New York Times, 1 August, p. 31.
       Lehmann-Haupt confesses he has difficulty in approaching Yellow Back Radio Broke-Down, as he feels this novel taps "life rhythms and experiences only blacks could understand." But he concludes: "Yellow Back Radio is staged for an audience in a mood to mock, to see monuments blown up. . . . But it's propaganda--or counter-propaganda. And propaganda is an esthetic that anyone can understand." The reviewer does not give an explicit definition of his term propaganda, nor does he offer much more in his review than a plot summary.

1969

31 LIPTON, LAWRENCE. "Wordwitching Whitey's West." <u>Los Angeles Free Press</u>, 5 September, p. 29.
    Finds that in <u>Yellow Back Radio Broke-Down</u>, Reed's "canvas is bigger, his language-inventions more daring" than in <u>Free-Lance Pallbearers</u>. "He ventures into prophetic hind-sight, rewriting the role of the Black man in what has been patriotically (and genocidely) called 'the winning of the West.'" Reed's style is called hang-loose, "which resembles the mosaic of a psychedelic trip more than it does the charted expectabilities of conventional prose fiction."

32 McKINNEY, RUTH ANN. "Wild West Made Wilder Funnier." <u>Ft. Worth</u> (Tex.) <u>Star</u>, 10 August, no pagination.
    <u>Yellow Back Radio Broke-Down</u> is "one of the funniest pieces of writing this year. . . . Those who are tuned in to the turned-on generation of novelists will find it wholly delightful."

33 MAYNARD, ROBERT C. "Insights." <u>Washington Post</u>, 4 August, no pagination.
    Maynard praises <u>Yellow Back Radio Broke-Down</u> and Reed. He finds Reed to be a talent of great ability able to "teach us that the rewards of imagination are finer than the rewards of truth, for truth is necessary root, but imagination is the flower." Maynard believes <u>Yellow Back Radio Broke-Down</u>, unlike <u>Free-Lance Pallbearers</u> will not go ignored by the literary community.

34 NORRIS, HOKE. "Voodoo on the Range: A Parody." <u>Chicago Daily News</u>, 16 August, no pagination.
    Indicates he does not know what to make of <u>Yellow Back Radio Broke-Down</u>. It is "altogether confusing, but entertaining and provocative." He also offers a limited plot summary.

35 O'BRIEN, JOHN. "Unfunny Satire." (Charleston, W. Va.) <u>Gazette</u>, 9 November, no pagination.
    O'Brien states tht <u>Yellow Back Radio Broke-Down</u> "is a surrealistic satire directed at the American establishment and generally it is a failure. It fails because satire is rather a bitter pill and if not coated with humor, it is unlikely to be swallowed."

1969

36   O'MEALLY, BOB. "Reed's Book a Gas." <u>Colonist</u> (20 November):
     3.
          Enthusiastic reaction to <u>Yellow Back Radio Broke-Down</u>.
     "Brother Ishmael Reed's new book . . . should be read every
     day, read aloud in class, in the bathroom, to children, at
     anti-war rallies. Copy from it for Christmas cards, for
     prayer meetings or to practice your own funky handwriting,
     'cause it's a boss-ass book."

37   PRYCE-JONES, DAVID. "First Novels." <u>Punch</u> 256 (29 January):
     179.
          Pryce-Jones finds <u>Free-Lance Pallbearers</u> too jokey,
     with techniques and clever language defeating the novel,
     which is, in the main, plotless: "Such plot as exists is
     part of the satire." He concludes: "his novel has no
     means of obtaining variety and pace. The pages are all
     alike . . . ." Excerpts reprinted in 1978.48.

38   SCHOTT, WEBSTER. "Antiwestern in a Black Black Vein." <u>Life</u>
     67 (15 August):12.
          Finds <u>Yellow Back Radio Broke-Down</u> to be written "from
     guts knotted with hostility toward white American history,
     Christian myth, liberal morality." Schott depicts the
     novel as nonsense filled with one-liners, powerless, ir-
     relevant. The only good pointed out is Reed's desire to
     be good. Schott is particularly distressed by the anti-
     novel, anti-hero, unconventional sense of time, and the
     lack of traditional satirical convention. He does find
     Reed good and black.

39   SHEPARD, WALT. "When State Magicians Fail: An Interview with
     Ishmael Reed." <u>Journal of Black Poetry</u> 1 (Summer-Fall):
     72-75.
          Reprint of 1968.8.

40   _____. "If the Indians Have Been Wiped Out, Then What Are All
     Those Drums?" <u>Nickel Review</u> (August):14.
          Reviewing <u>Yellow Back Radio Broke-Down</u>, Shepard finds
     that "whatever the autopsy of the American novel as we
     know it will show, Ishmael Reed is not waiting for the
     funeral to claim his inheritance." Shepard also notes
     that Reed overturns stone by stone the mythology of the
     wit as created by television: "Reed displays admirable
     courage at a time when the cultural politicians haunch,
     polishing rusty hatches, at the gates of a crumbling
     columbia; for this is a chronicle of a sacredcowless
     mooment" [<u>sic</u>].

1969

41   SINGER, H. BOB. "Yellow Back Radio Broke-Down." New York
      Herald Tribune, 28 September, p. 12.
          Enthusiastic discussion of Reed's first novel. Reed is
      called "wordsmith and taleteller extraordinaire" and is
      compared variously to Terry Southern, Donald Barthelme,
      William Burroughs, and Allen Ginsburg. Singer concludes
      that the novel is "the hippest, funniest, most inspired
      novel I have read in a long time, and I cant [sic] see
      anyone who loves life and literature missing it."

42   SISSMAN, L. E. "Books: Real and Unreal." The New Yorker
      (11 October):199-202.
          States a belief that Yellow Back Radio Broke-Down
      should be read, while at the same time taking exception to
      Reed's use of overt and covert sexuality. The reviewer
      asserts that Reed is too young a writer to undertake the
      job he did in this novel.

43   TEST, GEORGE A. "The Cliché as Archetype." Satire Newsletter
      7 (Fall):79.
          States that Reed has employed several levels of comment
      and indictments in Yellow Back Radio Broke-Down. "Whether,
      despite the validity of the indictment, we have here another
      version of the myth of the exotic primitive in touch with
      some rich unrecognized current of life is not altogether
      clear. What is clear is that Ishmael Reed is a very im-
      aginative and funny writer, well worth watching for."

44   VIGNEAULT, WILF. "Black But Not Caring." Montreal Star,
      13 September, no pagination.
          Discussion of Free-Lance Pallbearers and Yellow Back
      Radio Broke-Down. The two books "must be read. Not to
      read them is to be an ostrich, hoping that the scream of
      ghetto dwellers, both black and white, will either fade
      away or be muffled."

45   WINFREY, LEE. "Singalee and the Loop Garoo Kid: Western Will
      Never Be the Same." Detroit Free Press, 28 September, no
      pagination.
          Reviewing Yellow Back Radio Broke-Down, Winfrey finds it
      fascinating to watch the workings of the novel, "for
      Ishmael Reed is a Negro, and watching him at work in the
      lily-white world of the Western is like having Malcolm X
      describe the white johns he knew in his hustling days."

1970

46   WOODFORD, JOHN. "The Free-Lance Pallbearers." Negro Digest
      (February):68-69.
          Says Free-Lance Pallbearers is "good for several read-
      ings. He captures the familiar bathroom texture and odor
      of American life, and it is likely that the American 1984
      totalitarian society will, if it comes to that, bear a
      strong (in all senses of the word) resemblance to the world
      of The Free-Lance Pallbearers."

                             1970

1   ANON. "19 Necromancers From Now." Kirkus Reviews 38
      (15 August):933.
          Makes brief reference to the various portions of the
      collection, and advances this overall reaction: "this
      collection has an intriguing cadence and quality and a
      potent sense of style."

2   ANON. "Reed, Ishmael 1938- ." In Contemporary Authors: A
      Bio-Bibliographical Guide to Current Authors and Their
      Works. Edited by Barbara Harte and Carolyn Riley.
      Vol. 23/24. Detroit, Mich.: Gale Research Co., p. 348.
      Biographical and bibliographical listing.

3   ANON. "Reed--19 Necromancers." Bibliographic Survey: The
      Negro In Print 6 (November):7.
          Very brief notice, mentioning the publication of the
      work.

4   ANON. "Yellow Back Radio Broke-Down." Western Round-Up
      (January):no pagination.
          Warns this periodical's fans not to "be deceived into
      considering it [the novel] a 'western' nor a novel about a
      Black cowboy. . . . It is a profane, bawdy and horrifying
      and sustained bitter comedy for the tough in mind and
      spirit. It is also a curious and interesting exercise in
      an eccentric novelistic form."

5   FLEISCHER, LENORE. "Paperbacks: Non-Fiction." Publishers'
      Weekly 197 (29 June):105.
          Notes that 19 Necromancers From Now is also scheduled
      for publication in hardback by Doubleday, and that this is
      an important collection.

1970

6   GUINEY, ELIZABETH. "19 Necromancers From Now." Library
      Journal 95 (August):2683.
          Indicates that the content of excerpts from novels and
      plays are seen by Reed as coming from those Afro-Americans,
      Native Americans, and Chinese Americans who are "Necro-
      mancers and members of the movement of 'Neo-Hoodoism.'"
      No opinion is given as to the intrinsic value of the col-
      lection. The reviewer notes that the makeup of the various
      fragments is in "the ultra-absurdist vein."

7   HERNTON, CALVIN. "A Fiery Baptism." In Amistad I. Edited by
      John A. Williams and Charles F. Harris. New York: Vintage
      Books, pp. 200-25.
          Discusses several contemporary black authors. Reed
      (pp. 220-22) is likened to a hurricane: "You can hear him
      miles away before he arrives, and he arrives in seconds,
      for he is fast and he never misses." Free-Lance Pall-
      bearers and Yellow Back Radio Broke-Down are mentioned
      enthusiastically: "With these two novels [he] has shown
      himself to be the foremost heavyweight satirist of all
      times." Excerpts reprinted in 1978.48.

8   HOWE, IRVING. "Letters: Books in Black--Irving Howe
      Replies." Harper's Magazine 240 (March):6.
          Howe replies to Reed's response ("Letters," 1970) to
      Howe's review of Free-Lance Pallbearers (1969.15). "The
      one possibility that Mr. Reed seems unable to consider is
      that--unlike other young black novelists I did praise--he
      has not yet written a book worth taking seriously."

9   LESTER, JULIUS. "19 Necromancers From Now." Rolling Stone
      Magazine, no. 70 (12 November):44.
          Mentions several selections in the work as deserving
      notice. "Reed has put together an 'original' anthology
      that is worth checking out. Indeed, it is refreshing to
      see black writers presented for whatever merit they have
      as artists rather than for their political attitudes. The
      subjugation of art to politics is a crime against the hu-
      man consciousness. Reed's anthology is one shell, accu-
      rately fired, for the embattled artist."

10 LIPTON, LAWRENCE. "Is Black is Beautiful is Magic is Soul
      is--What?" Los Angeles Free Press, 7 (9 October), p. 33.
          Takes up the problems black writers and second genera-
      tion Jewish writers of the 30s and 40s have experienced by
      having their works misreviewed. Lipton notes that it is
      easier to review an anthology because the anthologist has

already made the selection. He quotes a great portion of
the introduction to 19 Necromancers From Now and smaller
portions from the anthology.

11 MIYAMOTO, YOKICHI. Translated from the Japanese by M. I.
Yamada. "New Trends in Black Literature." Asahi Shimbun
(9 February):no pagination.
    Surveys trends in black literature and took its impetus
from Irving Howe's article in 1969.28. Miyamoto, a
Japanese scholar of American literature, discusses Howe's
premise that the "characteristics shining through somewhat
raw techniques give ample indication of the new trend in
black literature which is bound to adorn the seventies."
One of the trend-setters is Ishmael Reed and his novel,
Yellow Back Radio Broke-Down.

12 SIMS, BENNETT. "Words: No Title." Three Days of Peace and
Music: Aquarian Exposition: Woodstock Music and Art Fair
August 15-17, 1970. Program notes, pp. 4-5.
    Mentions Reed, among others, as evidence that this gen-
eration is producing much literary material and reading it.

13 SKEETER, SHARYN J. "19 Necromancers From Now." Essence 1,
no. 8 (December):74.
    Very short notice. Describes the collection as "the
most contemporary, diverse, and prophetic collection of
American modern prose to be published to date."

14 WHITE, EDWARD M. "Story of Black Power Overcoming Evil."
Los Angeles Times Book Review, 25 January, p. 2.
    Offers a plot summary of Yellow Back Radio Broke-Down
and the statement that "more and more of the best new
American fiction is overly anti-realistic. This has been
an avant-garde truism since John Hawkes's The Cannibal
. . ." emerged as one of the guiding lights to reading
Yellow Back Radio Broke-Down. He also notes that the novel
is a satire directed at contemporary white society.

15 WRIGHT, ROBERT C. "Fiction." University of Denver Quarterly
(Spring):162-63.
    Reviews Yellow Back Radio Broke-Down noting that the
novel is the first of its genre: "The first American
Hoo-Doo Western." Wright finds the novel filled with
demonic images of the sort described by Northrop Frye in
his Anatomy of Criticism. Wright concludes, "hopefully
the book can help turn the country around so that the
creative side of May's demonic can come to the fore."

1971

1971

1   ANON. "A Casanova's Adventures in Post-War Germany."
    Halifax Evening Courier and Guardian (Yorkshire, Eng.),
    14 May, no pagination.
        Reed's Yellow Back Radio Broke-Down is one of several
    books reviewed in this piece. "It has a crazy theme, the
    characters are ludicrous, and the result, the first 'Hoo-
    doo' western, is uninhibited, astonishing, hilarious, and
    at some times shocking."

2   ANON. "Notes on Current Books." Virginia Quarterly Review
    47 (Winter):xv, xviii.
        Points out that from the dedication of 19 Necromancers
    From Now (to Chester Himes) to the collection of contribu-
    tors, "the young writers here practice a kind of 'magic
    naturalism,' a prophetic prose that claims to restore a
    primordial logos to descriptions of contemporary life."
    Further, this collection represents "some of the most
    dynamic prose being written today. Ishmael Reed, an im-
    portant talent in himself, contributes an exceptionally
    thoughtful introduction."

3   ANON. "Paperbacks." Black World 20 (August):92.
        Publication notice of 19 Necromancers From Now.

4   ANON. "West and South." Times Literary Supplement, 25 June,
    p. 726.
        A short review which notes that Yellow Back Radio Broke-
    Down is "a better organized and more confidently sustained
    novel [than Free-Lance Pallbearers]; its parodies less wild
    and consequently more destructively accurate . . . ."

5   ANON. "Yellow Back Radio Broke-Down." Evening Chronicle
    (Northumberland, Eng.), 5 June, no pagination.
        Short notice which asserts that the novel is a "shock-
    ing book in the best sense of the word." The reviewer
    states that "the book should really be read out loud by an
    expert in this arcane Black art of backchat." It concludes:
    "If you've got some imagination, some sympathy for the
    devil, read it. It's a good trip."

6   ANON. "Yellow Back Radio Broke-Down. Manchester Evening News
    (England), 26 May, no pagination.
        Brief publication notice. "It is easy to see that there
    is a talent behind this book . . . the difficulty is trying
    to make out what the talent is getting at. . . . Perhaps
    American readers will find it less gnomic."

1971

7 BRYANT, JERRY H. "Politics and the Black Novel." <u>Nation</u> 213
  (20 December):660-62.
   Finds <u>Yellow Back Radio Broke-Down</u> "significant," a
  novel in which "he may have begun a journey into a new form
  altogether, in which violence is exaggerated to the point
  of absurdity, in which our appetite for it is gratified but
  kept safely imaginary." The review also includes comment
  on several other books.

8 BURNS, JIM. "Send-up of the Western." <u>Tribune</u> (London),
  2 July, no pagination.
   <u>Yellow Back Radio Broke-Down</u> is "less hard-hitting [than
  <u>Free-Lance Pallbearers</u>] but it does effectively send-up one
  of the great American myths (the Western) and at the same
  time makes oblique comments on the contemporary scene."
  Burns concludes with a note of speculation: "He should be
  about ready to produce a book that really hammers home his
  caustic view of the world."

9 CARR, AUDREY. "Bizarre Americans in Violent Paris." <u>Evening
  Despatch</u> (County Durham, Ireland), 21 May, no pagination.
   Includes mention of <u>Yellow Back Radio Broke-Down</u>. "A
  sinister novel this, very amusing."

10 CRAWLEY, PHILLIP. "In Pursuit of Permissiveness." <u>Journal</u>
  (Northumberland, Eng.), 29 May, no pagination.
   <u>Yellow Back Radio Broke-Down</u> "is a savagely satirical
  send-up of every myth ever concocted about the Old West."
  Reed "has a wicked talent for the sort of surrealistic
  fantasy which . . . speaks volumes by inference about
  America's mortally sick society."

11 FENDERSON, LEWIS. "The New Breed of Black Writers and Their
  Jaundiced View of Tradition." <u>CLA Journal</u> 15 (September):
  18-24.
   Brief discussion of Reed. "What he calls a unique black
  contribution to modern art is Ishmael Reed's neo-hoodooism,
  an art form that the slaves brought to America."

12 FORD, NICK AARON. "A Note on Ishmael Reed: Revolutionary
  Novelist." <u>Studies in the Novel</u> 3 (Summer):216-18.
   Summarizes <u>Free-Lance Pallbearers</u> and <u>Yellow Back Radio
  Broke-Down</u>, and quotes from the latter as examples of
  philosophical and social overtones of the novel. <u>Free-
  Lance Pallbearers</u>, Ford asserts, "indicts American society,
  (thinly disguised) for its false morality, sexual degen-
  eracy, paternalism and imperialism (foreign and domestic),
  commercialism of religion, and maintenance of a color/
  caste system."

1971

13 HARRIS, CHARLES B. <u>Contemporary American Novelists of the</u>
    <u>Absurd</u>. New Haven, Conn.: College & University Press,
    p. 134.
        Includes Reed among the novelists who "treat absurdist
    themes with absurdist techniques."

14 KATZ, BILL. "<u>Don't Ask Me Who I Am</u>; and <u>catechism of d</u>
    <u>neoamerican hoodoo church</u>." <u>Library Journal</u> 96 (1 May):
    1617.
        In this brief notice, Katz believes that Reed's collec-
    tion is "too polemic, too forced." He says "What may pass
    as clever is often only dull," and concludes with "skip
    Reed."

15 LIPTON, LAWRENCE. "The Spectre of Neohoodooism is Haunting
    America." <u>Los Angeles Free Press</u>, 7 May, p. 26.
        Uses the occasion of the publication of <u>catechism of d</u>
    <u>neoamerican hoodoo church</u> to herald the coming popularity
    of pagan hoodooism as a direct challenge to the failing
    Judeo-Christian church: "The capitalist Establishment has
    good reason to panic and go genocidal. Their end is nearer
    than they think." Quotes "I am a Cowboy in the Boat of
    Ra."

16 M, J. W. "Black and White." <u>Huddersfield Daily Examiner</u>
    (England), 24 June, no pagination.
        <u>Yellow Back Radio Broke-Down</u> "is a strange and somewhat
    disturbing book. Though it has been well received by the
    American critics, we have still to see what effect it will
    have, if any, on this side of the Atlantic."

17 McBAIN, BARBARA MAHONE. "<u>catechism of d neoamerican hoodoo</u>
    <u>church</u>." <u>Black World</u> 20 (October):89-90.
        Brief favorable review of Reed's poetry.

18 MAJOR, CLARENCE. "<u>catechism of d neoamerican hoodoo church</u>."
    <u>Essence</u> 1 (March):61.
        Reviews Reed's first collection of poetry, noting that
    Reed has "assembled some of his finest poems. . . . (Per-
    sonally, my hope is that soon some alert publisher will
    bring out, in a proper way, a big book of his poems.)"

19 MEDWICK, LUCILLE. "The Afro-American Poet in New York."
    <u>New York Quarterly</u>, no. 6:102-18.
        Reed is seen as demonstrating the "bitterness and
    mockery in Afro-American poetry, sarcasm and ridicule."
    A short excerpt from Reed's poem "I Am a Cowboy in the
    Boat of Ra" is included.

20 MINUDRI, REGINA. "Books For Young Adults." <u>Library Journal</u>
       96 (15 May):1783.
          Brief notice in a list of books for the young adult, or
       teen, audience. "No one will like all of it [<u>19 Necro-
       mancers</u>] but everyone will like parts."

21 NESBITT, W. J. "Satire Time." <u>Northern Echo</u> (Durham, Eng.),
       21 May, no pagination.
          <u>Yellow Back Radio Broke-Down</u> is reviewed, among others.
       "I couldn't find much of anything in [the novel] either,
       despite a paean of praise from America. The comic strip
       style is not for me, and the theory that all experience is
       art seems justifiable only if you don't use the normal
       meaning of words, in the manner of Humpty Dumpty."

22 S., P. "Myth Killer." <u>Evening Post and Chronicle</u>
       (Lancashire, Eng.), 15 May, no pagination.
          Brief mention of <u>Yellow Back Radio Broke-Down</u>. "Ameri-
       can folk-lore will never be the same again."

23 SHEPARD, WALT. "When State Magicians Fail." In <u>Black
       Insights: Significant Literature by Black Americans 1760
       to the Present</u>. Edited by Nick Aaron Ford. Waltham,
       Mass.: Ginn & Co., pp. 304-9.
          Reprint of 1968.8.

24 SHRAPNEL, NORMAN. "The Eyes Have It." <u>Guardian Weekly</u> 104
       (22 May):19.
          Briefly describes <u>Yellow Back Radio Broke-Down</u> as
       "genuinely inventive, a black carnival in words."

25 _____. "When State Magicians Fail." In <u>Survival Prose: An
       Anthology of New Writings</u>. Edited by John Bart Gerald and
       George Blecher. New York: Bobbs-Merrill Co., pp. 151-63.
          Reprint of 1968.4.

26 STANFORD, DEREK. "The Double-VEnus Obsession." <u>Scotsman</u>
       (Edinburgh), 15 May, no pagination.
          Brief mention of <u>Yellow Back Radio Broke-Down</u>. "I do
       not feel Mr. Reed has been quite successful in his purpose,
       but there are plenty of semi-readers who will take his in-
       tentions for achievement."

27 STOREY, ELIZABETH. "<u>19 Necromancers From Now</u>." <u>Library
       Journal</u> 96 (15 January):288.
          Short review taking up books for youth, finds the col-
       lection is "for older kids, especially those interested in
       current trends in American literature."

1971

28   WOODS, EDDIE. "Compassionate View." <u>Morning Star</u> (London),
         10 June, no pagination.
             Brief notice of <u>Yellow Back Radio Broke-Down</u>. "You'll
         laugh too--that makes a change."

<u>1972</u>

1   ABEL, ROBERT H. "Reed's 'I Am a Cowboy in the Boat of Ra.'"
        <u>Explicator</u> 30, item 81.
            An attempt to explicate some of the buried allusions of
        an historical nature within Reed's poem. Abel provides
        some interesting material and offers some hypotheses as to
        the meaning of the poem. He also notes the connections
        between this poem and <u>Yellow Back Radio Broke-Down</u>.

2   AMBLER, MADGE. "Ishmael Reed: Whose Radio Broke Down?"
        <u>Negro American Literature Forum</u> 6:125-31.
            This review includes a reprinting of Reed's poem "I Am
        a Cowboy in the Boat of Ra," and notes that Reed is a poet
        first and a novelist second. Further, Ambler states that
        several of the themes in <u>Yellow Back Radio Broke-Down</u> are
        present in "I Am a Cowboy," hence the reason for the re-
        printing. Despite the fact that the article is largely a
        plot summary and a simple explication of the poem, it is
        interesting to note the various themes which recur in each
        of the works.

3   ANON. "Briefly Noted." <u>New Yorker</u> 48 (16 September):125.
            Suggests that <u>Mumbo Jumbo</u> is "a partly intelligible
        pastiche, much of it about an 'anti-plague called 'Jes'
        Grew.'"

4   ANON. "<u>Conjure</u>." <u>Book World</u> 6 (29 October):15.
            States that "Reed can be seen growing from a clever but
        derivative writer into a free-swinging man with a mind and
        a voodoo-jive language of his own."

5   ANON. "Ishmael Reed Explores His Unfinished Past." (Trenton,
        N.J.) <u>Sunday Times Advertiser</u>, 13 August, p. 7.
            Finds Reed "a mean man with a myth." Notes that <u>Mumbo
        Jumbo</u> is a sophisticated work: Reed might be categorized
        as a militant black writer but Reed "sees the war for black
        identity being fought not only between cop and kid and
        boss and worker but also between the powers of black life--
        music, magic, dance, ecstasy--and those of self-aggrandizing
        white rationalism."

1972

6   ANON. "Literature: Fiction." <u>World Progress</u> (Autumn):334.
        Short notice which calls <u>Mumbo Jumbo</u> "a blend of magic,
  hoodoo, history, detective story, humor, and jive."

7   ANON. "<u>Mumbo Jumbo</u>." <u>Booklist</u> 69 (15 September):69.
        Abbreviated publication notice.

8   ANON. "<u>Mumbo Jumbo</u>." <u>Kirkus Reviews</u> 40 (1 July):641.
        Summarizes as nearly as possible the basic premises of
  the novel and comments briefly on the "put downs" of certain parts of Western civilization. It concludes: "The
  fast, dense almost gnostic prose abounds with allusions to
  everything under (and over) the sun, and it is more than
  worth the difficulties the non-attuned or unitiated reader
  may have in following it."

9   ANON. "1972: A Selection of Noteworthy Titles." <u>New York
  Times Book Review</u>, 3 December, p. 78.
        Describes <u>Mumbo Jumbo</u> as "a conjurer of a book that will
  hoodoo you."

10   ANON. "Post Bookworm." <u>Post</u>, 12 October, p. 4.
        The review is a collage of quotations about <u>Mumbo Jumbo</u>
  from reviews in other sources. All of the sources quoted
  are available elsewhere in this bibliography.

11   ANON. "Television." <u>Jet Magazine</u> (November):66.
        Mentions Reed appeared on "Like It Is," an ABC-TV show.

12   ANON. "Who-Dun-It Leaves Reader Guessing Villian's [<u>sic</u>]
  Identity." <u>Fort Wayne News-Sentinel</u>, 16 September,
  p. 5WK.
        In <u>Mumbo Jumbo</u> Reed "writes with a certain satiric
  flavor but it frequently seems that his tongue is just a
  little too far back in his cheek. As a consequence, his
  words and the images they create are muddled and unclear."

13   AVANT, JOHN ALFRED. "<u>Mumbo Jumbo</u>." <u>Library Journal</u> 97
  (1 October):3182.
        Avant finds that this novel is like "a loose pop-version
  of Thomas Mann--not that <u>Mumbo Jumbo</u> is in that class, but
  its design is unusually vast for such a small funny book,
  and it's good entertainment most of the way."

1972

14 BAKER, HOUSTON A., Jr. "Books Noted." Black World 22
      (December):63-64.
        Notes that with his third novel, Reed has had his ar-
      tistic coming-of-age. Mumbo Jumbo, according to Baker,
      offers "a conspiracy view of history, a critical handbook
      for the students of the Black Arts, and a guide for the
      contemporary Black consciousness intent on the discovery
      of its origins and meanings." He further states that
      "Mumbo Jumbo is perhaps the first Black American novel of
      the last ten years that gives one a sense of the broader
      vision and the careful painful and laborious fundamental
      brainwork that [is] needed if we are to define the eternal
      dilemma of the Black Arts and work fruitfully toward its
      melioration." Excerpts reprinted in 1974.54.

15 BANNON, BARBARA. "Fiction." Publishers Weekly 201
      (19 June):57.
        Notice of Mumbo Jumbo in which the reviewer notes that
      "Reed has talent to burn, and there's never a dull moment,
      even when one doesn't quite know what's going on in the
      novel in the most literal terms."

16 BANNON, BARBARA A. "Writers in the West on the West."
      Publishers Weekly (9 October):67.
        Reed is included in an article mentioning writers who
      live in the West.

17 BREVARD, ROBERT S. "Conjure: Selected Poems, 1963-1970."
      Library Journal 97 (15 December):3992.
        Brevard states that Reed has "created an exceptional
      set of black-oriented poems. They represent a conscious
      production of an exclusively black aesthetic for American
      Negroes, which Reed calls Neo Hoo-Doo." He also notes that
      while longer poems are almost academic in style and struc-
      ture, understanding can only be accomplished by one well-
      versed in American ghetto lifestyle and Afro-American
      culture. The reviewer recommends Reed as one whose works
      belong in every American literature collection.

18 BRYANT, JERRY. "Who? Jes Grew? Like Topsy? No, Not Like
      Topsy." Nation 215 (25 September):245-47.
        In this substantial review, Bryant states that Mumbo
      Jumbo, unlike Reed's two previous novels, has "a somewhat
      more serious tone, and that is its main weakness. Reed
      becomes too much of an advocate of black glory. . . . Such
      self-congratulatory chest-thumping calls attention to it-
      self and undermines the satiric objectivity with which
      Reed approached his targets in his first two

1972

novels. . . . But on the whole, <u>Mumbo Jumbo</u> is an effective piece of satire. . . ." Bryant states that Reed is an historical novelist and <u>Mumbo Jumbo</u> in particular a novel which "has the texture of a weird history book." This review finds little basic fault with Reed's experiments, but does point out a few weak spots in the novel, dismissing them as minor flaws. Excerpt reprinted in 1978.48.

19 CASH, EARL A. "<u>Mumbo Jumbo</u>." <u>Best Sellers</u> 32 (1 October): 299.
    Emphasizes the potential danger of dismissing the book as "mumbo jumbo" or of claiming to understand it, either. He concludes that "A story that begins as a farce turns into one of dire earnestness, pleading the cause of black cultural uniqueness."

20 DAVIS, GEORGE. "Bright Blend of Mythology, History." <u>Philadelphia Inquirer</u>, 13 August, no pagination.
    Comments briefly, noting that Reed's style in <u>Mumbo Jumbo</u> w-s apparently presaged in his two previous novels. The review concludes with the assertion that "Reed's vision is clear. He has, like an 'anti-Freud' begun renaming things."

21 _____. "The 1920s Cultural War: <u>Mumbo Jumbo</u>." <u>Washington Post</u>, 4 August, Section B, p. 6.
    Identical to 1972.14.

22 DUNLAP, BRYAN. ". . . And Blacks Fighting For Special Identity." <u>Chicago Sun Times</u>, 6 August, no pagination.
    Dunlap finds Reed's exploration of the past in <u>Mumbo Jumbo</u> very worthwhile, and notes that the "intricate and profoundly funny world that Reed has created for his myths is worth exploring." Excerpts reprinted in 1974.54 and 1978.48.

23 EMERSON, O. B. "Cultural Nationalism in Afro-American Literature." In <u>The Cry of Home: Cultural Nationalism and the Modern Writer</u>. Edited by H. Ernest Lewald. Knoxville: University of Tennessee Press, pp. 235-38.
    Surveys trends, motives, and social forces surrounding Cultural Nationalism in Afro-American literature, including the usual important writers (Baldwin, Ellison, Bontemps, and Wright). Emerson also includes earlier writers such as Toomer, working his way historically to Reed. In the section concerning Reed, he finds that "the Afro-American novel reaches its highest achievement in Ishmael Reed, whose writing is the most unusual of all discussed in this

1972

essay." Emerson provides a plot summary of <u>Free-Lance Pallbearers</u> as well as excerpts from an interview between Walter Shepard and Ishmael Reed (1968.8).

24 FRANK, SHELDON. "Ishmael Reed and the 'Jes Grew' Plague." <u>Chicago Daily News</u>, 12 August, no pagination.
    Notes that Reed has moved away from the standard concerns of many contemporary black writers, and indicates that <u>Mumbo Jumbo</u> is a difficult novel in which Reed makes no concessions to his readers.

25 FRIEDMAN, ALAN. "Part Vision, Part Satire, Part Farce, Part Funferal." <u>New York Times Book Review</u>, 6 August, pp. 1, 22.
    Friedman points out that Ishmael Reed "has for some time now occupied a black out-post in a white landscape," and further, that <u>Mumbo Jumbo</u> is "a wholly original book [and] an unholy cross between the craft of fiction and witchcraft. . . . I mean that it attempts, through its deadpan phantasmagoria of a plot to achieve the kind of hold on its readers' minds that from ancient times and primitive contexts has always been associated with the secret Word, the Sacred Text." Friedman emphasizes that if the reader is willing to put aside preconceived notions of what a novel should be, <u>Mumbo Jumbo</u> begins to "establish a life of its own." It is more than just a novel, and beneath all the satire and plot machinations there lies an opposition between the gods, between Osiris and Aton. "There is a precedent, a novel once satiric and holy; <u>The Golden Ass</u> of Apuleius written for the ancient sect of Isis." Excerpts reprinted in 1974.54.

26 GAYLE, ADDISON, Jr. "Reed, Ishmael." In <u>Contemporary Novelists</u>. Edited by James Vinson. New York: St. Martin's Press, pp. 1053-54.
    Brief critical notice, with biographical and bibliographical information.

27 GORDON, ANDREW. "Spirits Abroad." <u>Saturday Review</u> 55 (14 October):76-78.
    Notes that <u>Mumbo Jumbo</u> is his best so far, and points out that it may "be destined to become a small classic of its kind. If so, is America in for another epidemic of 'Jes Grew'?" Excerpts reprinted in 1974.54.

28 HUNTER, STEPHEN. "Mumbo Jumbo Hoo-doos America." Baltimore
Sun, 13 August, no pagination.
Hunter finds Mumbo Jumbo inspired greatly by Vachel
Lindsay's poem "The Congo." But unlike the front page review of the novel in the New York Times Book Review, Hunter
finds the novel very conventional: the narration straight-
forward, the bizarre type fonts just scrambled newspaper
word games. Hunter's final comment: "In the end, Mr. Reed
offers little hope for a meeting of the cultures. . . .
Boomlay, boomlay, boomlay, BOOM."

29 JACOBS, THEODORE J. "A Few Novels." New Republic 167
(September):31.
Jacobs advances his belief that Mumbo Jumbo, along with
19 Necromancers From Now, attempts to set up the doctrine
of VooDoo.

30 LANE, GEORGE. "For Browsing and Drowsing." Patriot Ledger,
22 August, p. 12.
Lane finds Mumbo Jumbo has "a threat of sorts to it, a
prodigious and erudite bibliography and a kind of crazy
attraction for devotees of offbeat lore and for incurable
insomniacs."

31 LEE, ROBERT. "Cultures Clash in Mumbo Jumbo." Los Angeles
Times, 10 December, Calendar section, p. 78.
Asserts that beneath the comic aspects of the novel,
Reed is presenting a disturbing indictment of white Western
culture. Lee concludes that the revolution proposed in
Mumbo Jumbo would mean "inevitable separation between black
and white and the death of certain ways of thinking which
include the historical myths of America." But in the end
Lee suggests that the book should be read as comedy.

32 LEHMANN-HAUPT, CHRISTOPHER. "Decline and Fall of Jes Grew."
New York Times, 9 August, p. 35.
Points out that Mumbo Jumbo summarizes what the previous
works of Reed had been trying to say, namely "that the
African American cultural tradition that he [Reed] calls
Neo-HooDooism is alive and well and has roots going back to
pre-Christian times, when along came a cat named Moses who
stole The Book from the Temple of Osiris and Isis in Koptos
but got the message all wrong. All that tradition lacks
now is a Sacred Text, and if Mumbo Jumbo doesn't provide
it, Mr. Reed's next book might." While the overall tone of
the review is positive, Lehmann-Haupt does hold some reser-
vations about Reed's use of media to take Western European
culture to task.

1972

33 _____. "Jess Grew Threatens Uptight America." <u>Seattle Post-Intelligencer Book World</u>, 20 August, p. 17.
Calls <u>Mumbo Jumbo</u> "by far the best book Reed has yet written." Referring to the plot of <u>Mumbo Jumbo</u> Lehmann-Haupt states: "All of which adds up in its zany phantas-magoric way to more or less what Reed has been trying to tell us all along . . . that the Afro-American cultural tradition that he calls neo-hoodooism is alive and well and has roots going back to pre-Christian times."

34 McCABE, CAROL. "All Stirred Up Like Callaloo." <u>Providence</u> (R.I.) <u>Sunday Journal Leisure Weekly</u>, 12 November, p. H16.
McCabe reviews <u>Mumbo Jumbo</u>, finding its writer is "a very well-spoken black man." She finds the book angrier than <u>Yellow Back Radio</u> but also less mean than that work. In comparing Reed to Wolfe, she finds Reed writes even more from the ear, not using comic words such as 'Biff' and 'Pow,' but words like 'Mu'tafikah.'"

*35 MAJOR, CLARENCE. "The Explosion of Black Poetry." <u>Essence</u> 3, no. 2:44–47.
Cited in 1978.48.

36 _____. "<u>Mumbo Jumbo</u> by Ishmael Reed." <u>Black Creation</u> 4 (Fall):59–61.
Major extolls the novel: "Richer in detail than both <u>Yellow Back</u> and <u>Pallbearers</u>, <u>Mumbo Jumbo</u>—of the three novels—is more clearly conceived and more total, as an entity, in·effect. Though all three novels are fascinating works of original satire, <u>Mumbo Jumbo</u> has more color and sound. It is a word symphony in the spirit of freedom, joy, and passion; an elaborate composition in which all the elusive sonatas are the designs of an emotional understand-ing of history and human nature, justice and injustice; and, the book itself, once it is closed, stands in the mind—a challenge to the terms on which America's most popular mores and myths exist."

37 NORDELL, RODERICK. "Don't Stamp Out Krazy Kat." <u>Christian Science Monitor</u>, 6 September, p. 13.
Describes <u>Mumbo Jumbo</u> as a "cartoon with a brick in its hand." Nordell concludes that the novel is "its own sort of proof that Jes Grew has not been wholly stamped out."

38   OLDERMAN, RAYMOND M.   Beyond the Waste Land: A Study of the
      American Novel of the Nineteen Sixties. New Haven, Conn.:
      Yale University Press, p. 16.
          Mentions Reed as one among several who "parody the
      search for identity, admitting the seriousness of the
      problem but mocking our deadly earnest over-absorption in
      identity seeking."

39   PEARCE, GARY. "Mumbo Jumbo: Is It Brilliance or Garbage?"
      (Raleigh, N.C.) News and Observer, 3 September, Section IV,
      p. 6.
          After his opening assertion that "as much mumbo jumbo
      has been written about this book as was written in it,"
      Pearce answers the question posed in his review's title,
      saying that the work is "somewhere in the middle. A good,
      funny idea surrounded by too much garbage." He sums up:
      "Reed obviously has a great satiric touch. When he drops
      his bombs just right, they're devastating. And if he ever
      gets a lot of smarter bombs together in one book, that book
      will be devastatingly worth reading. So wait until his
      talent has jes' grewn a little bit."

39a   RITTER, JESS. "Minstrels' Memorial: Shreds of Patchen."
      Village Voice (9 March):pp. 20-21.
          Reports Reed's appearance and contribution to a memorial
      for Kenneth Patchen held at City Lights Poets Theatre.

40   SHEPPARD, R. Z. "Summer Fiction." Time 100 (14 August):67.
          Mumbo Jumbo is given notice in these terms: "It is a
      welcome alternative to the bludgeoning lectures of LeRoi
      (Imamu Baraka) Jones. Or is it? The club is a quicker
      and more merciful weapon than the feather."

41   TAYLOR, ROBERT. "A Cosmic Myth." Boston Globe, 22 August,
      no pagination.
          Mumbo Jumbo is "brilliant, phantasmal, eccentric and
      uneven . . . a visionary comic myth."

42   YOUNG, AL. "Interview: Ishmael Reed Part 1." Changes in
      the Arts, no. 78 (November):12-13, 33.
          This portion of the interview examines Reed's philo-
      sophical view of the world in the 1970s from a historical
      perspective, comparing with the 1920s.

1972

43   _____. "Mumbo Jumbo by Ishmael Reed." Changes (November):no
        pagination.
             Young calls Reed "the most original poet novelist work-
        ing in the American language." Mumbo Jumbo is a "prose-
        poetic gumbo." Young concludes that Reed has produced a
        "beautifully modulated work of art that's as meaningful as
        it is novel."

44   _____. "Simmered Prose, Poetic Gumbo." This World,
        3 September, no pagination.
             Young praises Mumbo Jumbo as "prose-poetic gumbo the
        ingredients of which have been painstakingly gathered, pre-
        pared and simmered over a low blue flame." The review also
        contains an extended plot summary.

                                1973

1   ANON. "Chattanooga." Kirkus Reviews 41 (1 August):867.
             Professes surprise at the work's tone: "more sober than
        his generally mind-blowing prose." The poems are "tersely
        written, with a fine tight rhythm, a complete lack of sen-
        timentality, plus a refreshingly idiosyncratic vision."

2   ANON. "Conjure." Choice 10 (May):460.
             Points out that Reed has received deserved critical
        acclaim for Pallbearers and Yellow Back Radio, but that
        this collection of poetry "suffers from the kind of ob-
        trusive polemicizing which permeates his most recently
        published work, Mumbo Jumbo." Further, the review states
        that the poetry too often "depends on typographical trick-
        ery (à la e. e. cummings) for effect."

3   ANON. "For the Future: LJ Takes Note." Library Journal 98
        (1 April):1198.
             Review of This One's On Me, which was withdrawn from
        publication and later reappeared as Shrovetide in Old New
        Orleans. This review makes reference only to the contents
        of the work: "The author . . . gives an account of his
        life. . . . Reed also includes in this book a number of
        short essays on a variety of subjects."

4   ANON. "Mumbo Jumbo." New Orleans Times Picayune,
        27 September, Section 2, p. 3.
             Notes that the novel is "a nostalgic, satirical, alle-
        gorical and sometimes confusing visit to a 1920s world."

5   ANON. "Notes on Current Books." Virginia Quarterly Review 49
     (Winter):viii, xvi.
         Finds that Mumbo Jumbo constitutes Reed's coming of age,
     and also notes that Reed's is the work of an artist of
     "amazing talent," and that the novel will have an overall
     effect of "flourishing genius on the minds and emotions of
     those who carry 'Jes Grew.'" The review also mentions
     Conjure, alluding to links between Reed's prose and
     poetry. The reviewer states that Reed is moving away from
     just a black stance into the realm of "Neo Hoo Doo."

6   ANON. "Reed, Ishmael. Mumbo Jumbo." Choice 10 (March):97.
         Asserts that Mumbo Jumbo is "a disappointment. True,
     it is a highly imaginative creation which periodically dis-
     plays great energy and incisive satire, but its weaknesses
     outweigh its strengths." A few sentences later, the re-
     viewer states a belief that the novel is "a racist polemic
     on the black cultural resurgence of the Harlem Renaissance."

7   ANON. "A Selected Vacation Reading List." New York Times
     Book Review, 10 June, p. 41.
         Very brief notice of Conjure. Indicates that the
     poetry's "rhythms are derived from the black militant
     underground and controlled with exceptional craft and
     discipline."

8   ANON. "West Coast Books." Newsweek (19 February):83-84.
         Discussion of publishing trends on the West Coast.
     Calls Reed "one of the most important black novelists" and
     mentions his publishing activities in Berkeley.

9   AUBERT, ALVIN. "Chattanooga." Library Journal 98
     (15 September):2556.
         States that "Reed's fiction and poetry are an organic
     whole and should be read in toto along with his 'manifesto'
     for a full comprehension of any part of 'hoo doo' as the
     secret of black people's survival in the West and of their
     future prominence in surviving a dying civilization. . . .
     Strong prose with a 'left hook out of nowhere.'"

10   BEAR NEBULA [pseud.]. "Hoodoos Levitate Moon." Beloit
     College Newspaper, 24 May, no pagination.
         Suggests that for understanding of Neo-Hoodooism and the
     Neo-Hoodoo Church at Beloit readers should take up Mumbo
     Jumbo and Yellow Back Radio Broke-Down.

1973

11 BEAUFORD, FRED. "Conversation with Ishmael Reed." <u>Black</u>
    <u>Creation</u> 4:12-15.
        This interview/essay contains some interesting bio-
    graphical material. More importantly, Reed discusses his
    intentions in writing <u>Mumbo Jumbo</u>.

*12 BLUFORD, KEN. "Clarence Major: The Enormousness of Real
    Art." (Philadelphia) <u>Drummer</u>, 29 May, p. 11.
        Cited in 1978.48.

13 BOITANI, PIERO. <u>Prosatori Negri Americani Del Novecento</u>.
    Rome: Edizioni di Storia e Letteratura, pp. 268-72.
        Boitani discusses many Black American authors. Reed's
    <u>Free-Lance Pallbearers</u> is described as having its basis in
    "the satirical-grotesque distortion of American reality.
    . . . The more frequent impression is that playing with
    slang . . . may too often be an end in itself. <u>Free-Lance</u>
    <u>Pallbearers</u> is therefore a promising novel, but not quite
    a successful one." Briefly makes comparisons of Reed with
    Ellison and Baraka. In Italian. Excerpt reprinted in
    1978.48.

14 BRYANT, JERRY H. "Lights and Laughter Everywhere." <u>Nation</u>
    216 (19 March):378.
        Discusses the first volume of <u>Yardbird Reader</u> and the
    purpose of the Yardbird Cooperative. Bryant notes that the
    <u>Reader</u> was a little ragged, pointing out the fact that it
    had more than the average number of typographical errors.
    Bryant also points to the poor-quality writing even though
    that writing comes from such established writers as Claude
    Brown and Cecil Brown. However, he concludes by saying
    "the merits of this collection outweigh its weaknesses."

15 CASH, EARL. "The New Black Novel." <u>Cross Currents</u> 23 (Fall):
    339-42.
        Cash reviews and compares Reed's <u>Mumbo Jumbo</u> with John
    A. Williams's <u>Captain Blackman</u>. Both are to him examples
    of the new black novel whose purpose is to provide his-
    torical information essential for black survival. Reed's
    work provides an attempt at cultural preservation. The
    novel "contains a wealth of information which Blacks need
    to know, but is more enigmatic." He sums his review:
    "These are not one-dimensional narratives, but represent
    highly imaginative ways of presenting messages too timidly
    dealt with before."

16   DILLINGHAM, THOMAS. "Ishmael Reed. Chattanooga." Open
      Places 18 (Fall):58-60.
           In a review which includes extensive excerpts from the
      poems of Chattanooga, Reed is compared to Countee Cullen:
      "It should be no disservice to Cullen's work to compare him
      with a black poet writing today--a poet who has abandoned
      the anglicized rhythms, the 'poetic' images, and most of
      all the solemn tones of the past for a language all his
      own."

17   GAGA. "Interview with Ishmael Reed." Mwendo (Coe College,
      Cedar Rapids, Iowa), no. 4 (Fall):[32-35].
           Discusses general topics concerning Reed's impact and
      literary contribution.

18   GIFFORD, THOMAS. "New Fiction." Minneapolis Tribune,
      7 January, no pagination.
           Mumbo Jumbo is manifestly readable largely due to Reed's
      "highly personal handling . . . and the fact that Reed is
      very clever, very funny, and a wonderful relief from ten-
      dentious boors like Leroi Jones, or whatever he is pres-
      ently calling himself." Gifford sums up his review calling
      the novel a "stylish piece of work."

19   GROSSMAN, RICHARD. "Mumbo Jumbo by Ishmael Reed." San
      Francisco Phoenix (13 June):no pagination.
           The novel is a "masterful attack upon life in the white
      western world," one "which is determined to attack all
      writers/makers of history who have always overlooked events
      which did not take place in a royal audience chamber or a
      corporate board room." Grossman calls Reed nasty, a
      brilliant satirist, a militant with a sense of humor, and
      sums up: "He can write. This is an important book."

20   HAZO, SAMUEL. "Literature: American Fiction." Britannica
      Book of the Year. Chicago: Encyclopedia Britannica, Inc.,
      p. 424.
           In a short review of the year's output of American
      fiction, Reed's Mumbo Jumbo earns notice. It is charac-
      terized as a "singular experience" with "an incredible plot
      that defies summary, and a richness of verbal style that
      resists comparative analysis." Mumbo Jumbo "would cer-
      tainly, in time, locate Reed at the forefront of black
      American writers."

Writings about Ishmael Reed

1973

21   HASSAN, IHAB. "American Literature." In World Literature
     Since 1945: Critical Surveys of the Contemporary Litera-
     ture of Europe and the Americas. Edited by Ivar Ivask and
     Gero von Wilpert. New York: Frederick Ungar, pp. 1-64.
        Reed is mentioned (pp. 48, 61) in an overview discussion
     of American literature.

22   _____. Contemporary American Literature 1945-1972: An Intro-
     duction. New York: Frederick Ungar, pp. 77, 137, 172-73.
        Brief notice in survey of significant figures in modern
     American literature.

23   HEYER, WILLIAM. "Four Realities." Poetry (Chicago) 122
     (July):237-40.
        Points out that "The Jackal-Headed Cowboy," "The
     Gangster's Death," and "I Am a Cowboy in the Boat of Ra"
     are "nasty, and major poems." Heyer states that Conjure
     is an "outpouring of spirit, and exorcism."

24   HOEKSMA, THOMAS. "Fiction." Books Abroad 47 (Spring):367-68.
        The reviewer declares that in Mumbo Jumbo Reed has re-
     stored "a mutilated religious heritage, reveals the
     creative possibilities of magic, Satan, witchcraft, evil
     and the unknown, and initiates a new priesthood of Afro-
     American artists into the mysteries of their own past."
     Excerpt reprinted in 1975.45.

25   JOHNSON, HERSCHEL. "Mumbo Jumbo by Ishmael Reed." Black
     Enterprise 3 (January):46-47.
        Discusses the novel in terms of the influence religion
     (voodoo) has had on Reed's work, asserting that "the major
     power source of his material [has] been religion [specifi-
     cally, voodoo]." He states that examination along these
     lines gives insight as to "why Reed's work is among the
     most incisive being produced in any idiom by any writer
     today." Johnson thinks that Reed's central point in
     Mumbo Jumbo is "that dance has a strong spiritual and cul-
     tural history for black people, that it was integrally con-
     nected to religion, and through religion to politics, and
     that it was a great generative source of power." He con-
     cludes: "At any rate, he is handling all of it, black and
     white, tit for tat, and, well now, who says the cakewalk
     can't pull coat tails?"

68

26 LAMMING, GEORGE. "<u>Conjure</u>." <u>New York Times Book Review</u>,
6 May, p. 36.
This review of Reed's work also discusses <u>Another Life</u>
by Derek Walcott. Lamming finds Reed has "already con-
solidated his reputation as one of those black writers who
refuses to be categorized according to the relevance of his
theme." Excerpt reprinted in 1975.45 and 1978.48.

27 LEE, DEBORAH. "<u>Conjure</u> by Ishmael Reed." <u>Ebony</u> (March):no
pagination.
Finds the volume to be a "black magical selection. . . .
The beauty of Reed's poetry (and some poetic prose) is that,
in sharing with us, he reveals a remarkable finesse with
traditional forms as well as startling image-making powers."

28 McLELLAN, JOSEPH. "Paperbacks: Fiction--<u>Mumbo Jumbo</u> by
Ishmael Reed." <u>Book World</u> 7 (16 September):13.
Very brief notice. <u>Mumbo Jumbo</u> is "nostalgic, satiri-
cal, allegorical and sometimes confusing."

29 _____. "Paperback Shelf: <u>Mumbo Jumbo</u> by Ishmael Reed." <u>New</u>
<u>Orleans Times Picayune</u>, 27 September, Section 2, p. 3.
Reprint of 1973.28.

30 MEINKE, PETER. "On Five Poets." <u>New Republic</u> 169
(24 November):25.
This is a short review of <u>Chattanooga</u>, with Reed's section about 340 words long. Meinke finds both "Railroad
Bill" and "I am a Cowboy in the Boat of Ra" to be quite
good pieces. Further, he believes Reed is not as experimental as would first appear.

31 MIYAMOTO, YOKICHI. Translated from the Japanese by M. I.
Yamada. "Development of American Vanguard Literature."
<u>Asahi Shimbun</u> (30 June):7.
Discusses the changes and development of experimental
American literature comparing Kerouac, John Burns, and
Ishmael Reed. It attempts an historic approach to the
non-mainstream writings of the late twentieth century, and
adroitly points up the influences on each of these
writers. The review discusses Reed's <u>Mumbo Jumbo</u>.

32 NORRIS, RUTH. "The Black Poet Ishmael Reed Lashes Out in All
Directions." <u>Daily World</u>, 11 July, p. 8.
Reviewing <u>Conjure</u>, Norris finds Reed's vision clouded.
His conclusion is based on Reed's voice, which "says much
that is valid without understanding the class relation-
ships which are responsible for his frustration."

33   O'BRIEN, JOHN, ed. Interviews with Black Writers. New York:
       Liveright, pp. 165-83.
             Reprinting of 1973.24. See also 1975.42.

34   _____. Introduction [to interview with Ishmael Reed]. In
       Interviews with Black Writers. New York: Liveright,
       pp. 165-67.
             Notes that Reed is after a revolution of the imagination
       in his own fiction.

35   O'BRIEN, JOHN. "Ishmael Reed: An Interview." Fiction
       International 1 (Summer):61-70.
             In this interview, conducted prior to the publication
       of Mumbo Jumbo, Reed characterizes his novel in these
       terms: "As a matter of fact I call it my 'straight' book
       because I found it necessary to show people . . . I wasn't
       one of those 1960's put-on people." Reed also discusses
       how he attempts to draw characterization as capturing that
       essential quality of people and working that quality into
       his characterization. The interview is important for
       Reed's assessment of his own work and for his revelation
       of some of his sources of influence, including Nathanael
       West's The Dream Life of Balso Snell. Excerpt reprinted
       in 1977.29.

36   O'CONNELL, SHAUN. "Arts in Review--American Fiction, 1972:
       The Void in the Mirror." Massachusetts Review (Winter):
       190-207.
             The section on Reed (pp. 200-201) in this broad survey
       consists of approximately 160 words. Basically, O'Connell
       finds himself unable to understand Mumbo Jumbo, although
       he admits that he was caught up in it.

37   ROBINSON, EUGENE. "Reed: Chronicling the Black Spirit."
       Michigan Daily, 14 October, p. 4.
             Discussion of Mumbo Jumbo. Robinson believes that
       Reed's novels "would be totally irrelevant if not for the
       fact that they always eventually make a point." Reed is
       viewed as "the liveliest and most significant black novel-
       ist writing today." The reviewer urges a reading of the
       poetry in the context of the novels. "They [the poems]
       begin to make sense, establish a pattern, describe a black
       spiritualism too multifaceted and diffuse to explicate
       here."

1973

38   SCARBROUGH, GEORGE. "Chattanooga by Ishmael Reed."
      (Chattanooga, Tenn.) Times, 18 November, no pagination.
           Scarbrough reviews Chattanooga and finds only two poems
      worthy of note: "Railroad Bill, A Conjure Man" the best,
      and the title poem quite good. Otherwise, the poems are of
      the usual variety: "language shrewd, hard, streetwise;
      sometimes childish, always knowledgeable. Nothing jolting
      here."

39   SCHMITZ, NEIL. "The Poetry of Ishmael Reed." Modern Poetry
      Studies (Autumn):218-21.
           This review takes to task the selection of poetry in
      Conjure, finding Reed, "as the advocate of Neo-Hoo Doo,
      . . . a less significant poet."

40   THOMAS, LORENZO. "Books: The Black Roots are Black."
      Village Voice 18 (15 March):19+.
           Thomas attempts to relate aspects of contemporary life
      with realities of life shown in Mumbo Jumbo. While this
      review is written in a colloquial style, it has much to
      say and gives a good understanding of and insights into
      Mumbo Jumbo.

41   _____. "Neo Hoo Doo: The Sound Science of Ishmael Reed."
      University Review 29 (May):15-17, 28-30.
           A far-reaching essay which discusses several of Reed's
      novels, and his book of poetry, Conjure. "He speaks to
      those who are prepared to take the brunt of the mysteries
      and realize the future is coming from right here."

42   WHITLOW, ROGER. "Ishmael Reed." In Black American Litera-
      ture: A Critical History. Chicago: Nelson Hall,
      pp. 154-57.
           Contains a partial reprint of "I am a Cowboy in the Boat
      of Ra" and partial summaries of Free-Lance Pallbearers and
      Yellow Back Radio Broke-Down. Whitlow assesses Reed as a
      satirist in the absurdist tradition (whether of the ilk of
      Theatre d'Absurd or in the tradition of Mailer, Salinger,
      or Heller), who does more than point to the absurdity of
      American life. Reed uses that tradition "(to teach?
      perhaps somewhat) but mainly to amuse, to entertain--and
      entertain he does."

43   YOUNG, AL. "Interview: Ishmael Reed, Part 2." Changes in
      the Arts (December/January):21+.
           Concentrates on the problems of black, or minority,
      artists and the constraints of the current economic
      situation.

1974

1   ANON. "Briefly Noted: Fiction." New Yorker 50 (4 November):
      208-9.
          In Reed's portion of this survey, barely a paragraph
      long, the reviewer finds Last Days of Louisiana Red "a lot
      less funny and a lot more self-conscious" than Mumbo Jumbo.

2   ANON. "Chattanooga." Choice 7 (September):944.
          This is an eighty-word notice. "The poems are per-
      functory, low key, predictable, forgettable. Get his
      anthology, 19 Necromancers From Now (1970) instead of this
      one." The reviewer believes that Reed is an "editor of
      note" and that is "probably where his greatest literary
      value lies."

3   ANON. "Chattanooga's Poems." Booklist 70 (15 February):628.
          Finds that the title poem shows "an inexhaustible
      imagination."

4   ANON. "Hoodooism Enlivens Poet's Works." University Daily
      Kansan, 20 September, p. 8.
          A news story about Reed's reading at the University of
      Kansas as well as his stay as a member of the University's
      "writer-in-residence" program. The article touches briefly
      on some of Reed's ideas.

5   ANON. "The Hot Dark Prose of Ishmael Reed." People 2
      (16 December):50-52.
          A news story which discusses the many achievements of
      Reed including his nomination for the National Book Awards
      in two separate categories within the same year.

6   ANON. "Ishmael Reed." In Afro-American Encyclopedia.
      Vol. 8. North Miami, Fla.: Educational Book Publishers,
      pp. 2190-93.
          Narrative biographical essay.

7   ANON. "Last Days of Louisiana Red." Booklist 71 (1 Decem-
      ber):367.
          Finds Last Days "crafty, exhilarating and demanding."

8   ANON. "The Last Days of Louisiana Red." Burlington Free
      Press, 5 November, p. 16.
          The reviewer defines Last Days of Louisiana Red as a
      "funny takeoff on the cults, movements, and events of the
      immediate past--protest movements, women's lib, black

1974

studies . . . and especially the various stereotypes of
the black man in America during the past 40 years."

9   ANON. "The Last Days of Louisiana Red." Cultural Information
      Service (December):14.
          Calls the novel "a stylistic casserole of satire, alle-
      gory, mythology, and magic." It is a "fabulation about
      oppression, apathy, illusion, and the possibilities for
      renewal from within the black community. Whether blacks
      will take this tale to heart is not certain. But one
      can't help but be immensely impressed with Reed's inimi-
      table style."

10   ANON. "Last Days of Louisiana Red." Kirkus Reviews 42
      (15 August):899.
          Enthusiastic notice of Last Days, a book that "only
      Ishmael Reed, with his enormous post-rational leaps of
      causality, could devise." Reed is characterized as "a
      very important novelist."

11   ANON. "The Last Days of Louisiana Red." Pacific Sun Quar-
      terly (14 November-20 November):no pagination.
          Two-sentence publication notice of the novel.

12   ANON. "Playboy after hours: Books." Playboy 21 (November):
      25.
          This short review of Last Days of Louisiana Red notes
      that "the Black/white, man/woman power structures in the
      invisible empire are formulated more than explored, and the
      final icing on the cake is astrology. It must have been
      fun to write."

13   ANON. "Poet Reed at Brockport." Buffalo Evening News,
      1 April, p. 23.
          Announcement of Reed's appearance in Brockport.

14   ANON. "The Revised Amos and Andy." Sun, 10 November, p. D6.
          The reviewer finds The Last Days of Louisiana Red
      "duplicates the dizzying tempo of contemporary political
      and cultural systems." And like Thomas Pynchon, Reed has
      "a particular talent for assimilating into his novels
      erudition on many subjects and doing it with such a witty
      perversity that things rarely, if ever, seem heavy handed."

1974

15   AVANT, JOHN ALFRED. "Last Days of Louisiana Red." Library
     Journal 99 (1 December):3147-48.
          This short review, primarily a plot summary, finds Reed
     to be "at the very least a major stylist and one wants
     more."

16   BAILEY, LEAONEAD PACK, comp. Broadside Authors and Artists:
     An Illustrated Biographical Directory. Detroit, Mich.:
     Broadside Press, pp. 100-101.
          Routine biographical listing.

17   BANNON, BARBARA. "Fiction." Publishers Weekly 206
     (16 September):52.
          The reviewer comments that Reed is "at his bravura best
     in use of language and parody" in The Last Days of Louisiana
     Red.

18   BELL, PEARL K. "Writers and Writing: Black Magic." New
     Leader 57 (23 December):10.
          The reviewer believes Reed has talent and is inventive,
     but asserts that in The Last Days of Louisiana Red, "one
     can only lament the fact that . . . he has sacrificed his
     considerable gifts on the worthless altar of glib indo-
     lence." Excerpt reprinted in 1976.63.

19   BELLAMY, JOE DAVID, ed. "Ishmael Reed." In The New Fiction:
     Interviews with Innovative American Writers. Urbana:
     University of Illinois Press, pp. 130-41.
          This interview, conducted between the printing of Mumbo
     Jumbo and first release of that novel, gives Reed the op-
     portunity to explain that the way Mumbo Jumbo and others of
     his novels are edited reflects, in their speed and in the
     way their plots move, the influence television has had on
     his life. He also explains that his notion of Mumbo Jumbo
     as his "straight" novel means that he was using a "straight"
     form, that of the detective novel. Reed also gives a very
     detailed explanation of some of the media pieces in Mumbo
     Jumbo, as well as some of the incidents in that novel.
     Excerpt reprinted in 1977.29.

20   BROCK, MIKE. "New Year's Eve 1974." Oakland Tribune,
     29 December, p. 1-RAP.
          Reed, among several others, tells his plans for New
     Year's Eve. "He's planning to stay home . . . and digest
     what he called an old-fashioned Afro-American tradition--a
     Hoodoo Dinner. . . . Reed writes a new work every New
     Year's Eve."

1974

21   BRYANT, JERRY H.   "Ellison and Something New." Nation 218
     (25 May):663-64.
         Bryant compares a recent collection of critical articles
     written about Ralph Ellison to Yardbird Reader 2. He
     finds, in comparison, Yardbird Reader a fresh and exciting
     volume. He notes that Yardbird has some slight technical
     flaws, but the value of the whole is that it presents a
     sense of community: a community of artists who want to
     pursue their individual drafts rather than indulge in
     polemics for polemics' sake.

22   BUSH, ROLAND E.   "Werewolf of the Wild West: On a novel by
     Ishmael Reed." Black World 23 (January):51-52, 64-66.
         An intensive review of Yellow Back Radio Broke-Down.
     An interview with Reed is included in the article in which
     Reed expresses how he views his first novel, The Free-Lance
     Pallbearers. The interview also continues the Reed-Baldwin
     argument as Reed asserts of Baldwin's writings: those
     Jewish books that James Baldwin wrote. . . ." Reed dis-
     cusses influences on writers today: "a writer can be
     influenced by all kinds of media. You can pick it up from
     T.V. You don't have to read a single book." The reviewer
     acknowledges Reed's indebtedness to Marshall McLuhan's
     Electronic Age. Excerpt reprinted in 1975.45.

23   CAMPENNI, FRANK.   "Solid Gumbo vs. Louisiana Red." Milwaukee
     Journal, 29 December, no pagination.
         Reviews The Last Days of Louisiana Red and finds it the
     best Reed novel to date. Summing the novel's impact,
     Campenni states: "Interestingly, Reed dishes up his spicy
     compound of African and Greek legend, contemporary American
     and black slavery, so that you take it and like it."

24   COHRS, TIMOTHY.   "Hoodoos Howl at Reed Insult." Beloit
     College Round Table, 13 October, no pagination.
         Letter to the editor in response to an article by Joe
     Byrne, "Jesus versus the Voodoo Howlers." Includes quotes
     from "The Neo-HooDoo Manifesto."

25   COLTER, CYRUS.   "Red-hot gumbo-jumbo by Ishmael Reed."
     Chicago Daily News, 26 October, no pagination.
         Asserts at the outset: "a reviewer can't afford so
     strict a standard for a writer whose work he is assessing
     [which] may be attempting something wholly alien to the
     reviewer's experience and sensibility." Colter notes that
     Reed is a free spirit who "does his own thing, which shows
     confidence and even greater promise. To him, then--
     salute." Colter reviews The Last Days of Louisiana Red.

1974

26   CONNELL, CHRIS. "Author Sees Slur Against Voodoo in
     'Exorcist.'" (Bergen County, N.J.) Record, 22 April, no
     pagination.
          A newspaper article reporting Reed's dismay with the
     "Exorcist" and its swipes at voodoo, the front page review
     of Mumbo Jumbo in the New York Times Book Review, and the
     inclusion of Reed's poetry in the Norton Anthology. Also
     contains biographical material.

27   _____. "'Equal Time' Asked for Voodoo: Poet Dismisses
     'Exorcist' as Propaganda." Philadelphia Inquirer,
     11 April, no pagination.
          A news story concerning Reed's objection to a San Fran-
     cisco Roman Catholic priest's derogatory remarks on televi-
     sion concerning voodoo. Within the story is a short bio-
     graphical section and mention of Mumbo Jumbo as well as the
     appearance of Reed's poetry in The Norton Anthology of Poetry.

28   DALKE, JEFF. "Hoodooism and Psychic Distress." Richmond
     (Va.) Mercury, 6 November, pp. 16-17.
          Discusses The Last Days of Louisiana Red with reference
     to Reed's neo-hoodooism and to the Antigone myth. Dalke
     concludes that "the strengths of Reed's writing are
     caricature and cartoon. Each character is a stick with a
     slogan and relationships are typological. . . . The vir-
     tues acquired by this method are the degree to which
     abstract ideas can be made concrete and the emphasis that
     can be put on storytelling."

29   DAVIS, ARTHUR P. From the Dark Tower: Afro-American Writers
     1900-1960. Washington, D.C.: Howard University Press,
     p. 228.
          Mention of Reed: "Other [novelists] like . . . Ishmael
     Reed . . . show degrees of blackness varying from very
     little to none at all."

30   DREYER, PETER. "New Fiction: Brautigan, Gold and Reed."
     San Francisco 16 (December):86-87.
          Dreyer claims, in his review of The Last Days of
     Louisiana Red, that "the story defies summary." On the
     whole, Dreyer finds "Ishmael Reed . . . goes out too far
     on his limb, presumes too much of the reader, makes too
     little effort of identification."

31   DREYFUSS, JOEL. "Ishmael Reed, Speaking Out." Washington
     Post, 17 November, Section M, p. 1.
          Reed comments briefly on various aspects of his work,
     such as style and the success of his books. It is a sum-
     mary of Reed's major ideas and concepts.

32 DUFF, GERALD. "Reed's The <u>Free-Lance Pallbearers</u>."
    <u>Explicator</u> 32, item 69.
       Points to Reed's use of parody of Ellison's <u>Invisible</u>
    <u>Man</u>, the juncture being the grandfather's advice to the
    protagonist in <u>Invisible Man</u> and the maternal advice to
    Harry Sam in Reed's novel.

33 DURHAM, JOYCE ROBERTA. "The City in Recent American Litera-
    ture: Black on White: A Study of Selected Writings of
    Bellow, Mailer, Ellison, Baldwin and Writers of the Black
    Aesthetic." Ph.D. dissertation, University of Maryland.
       Discusses how contemporary black and white authors have
    come to terms with the city and imaginatively created that
    environment in their fiction. With writers in the sixties
    such as Reed, the image of the city in fiction, as well as
    the reality it purports to poetry, has made a gradual
    change from black on white to black and white.

34 EARLEY, JANE F. "A Strange 'Business.'" <u>Minneapolis Tribune</u>,
    10 November, p. 10D.
       Reviews <u>The Last Days of Louisiana Red</u> and finds that
    "whatever it is he is selling, Reed caters to an elite
    which will appreciate the reality of the collage he creates
    in lieu of Europeanized synthetic wares."

35 FOOTE, BUD. "Reed Ladles Out a Rich, Hot Gumbo." <u>National</u>
    <u>Observer</u> 13 (30 November):23.
       Discusses his experiences with Reed's works: "Reed's
    novels are always almost about anything, as near as I can
    figure out." Foote offers a plot summary of <u>The Last Days</u>
    <u>of Louisiana Red</u>.

36 GILDEA, WILLIAM. "Voices of Freedom Protesting." <u>Washington</u>
    <u>Post</u>, 30 April, pp. B1, B9.
       Notice of a poetry reading by Allen Ginsburg and Ishmael
    Reed at the Coolidge Auditorium of the Library of Congress.
    In an interview, Reed says he is committed to "showing that
    there is a tradition of Afro-American culture in this
    country, that Afro-Americans just didn't start writing.
    . . . The time extends backwards as new research comes in."
    Reed also says that he cannot get the "Hollywood establish-
    ment to understand and finance a film version of <u>Yellow</u>
    <u>Back Radio Broke-Down</u> but that others are raising the money
    and that it eventually will be a film." Daniel Hoffman,
    the consultant in poetry to the Library of Congress, says
    of Reed that he "has explored the fullness of the black
    tradition--all of its artistic experiences and expressions,
    including the folklore and songs of African slavery times

1974

as well as the life of the contemporary black, which he so well understands."

37 GORDON, ANDREW. "Ishmael Reed." City 4 (23 January-5 February):21-29.
    Surveys Reed's career and his major books to date.

38 HOLT, PAT. "Humorous Modern Novel of Black Voodoo." San Francisco Chronicle, 29 December, no pagination.
    Notes that this novel, The Last Days of Louisiana Red, "is one of the extraordinary novels to come along in a long time . . . it is a brilliant, original [novel] comparable to the best of Orwell and Huxley."

*39 IWAMOTO, IWAO. Gendai no America Shosetsu: Tairitsu to Mosaku. Tokyo: Eichosha.
    Cited in 1978.48.

40 JACKSON, BLYDEN, and RUBIN, LOUIS D., Jr. Black Poetry in America: Two Essays in Historical Interpretation. Baton Rouge: Louisiana State University Press, p. 88.
    Includes Reed in list of "black poets much in step with current modes."

41 KAISER, ERNEST. "Reed, Ishmael. The Last Days of Louisiana Red." Freedomways (Winter):379.
    Brief comments. "Reed must quit this kidding and mature and write novels concerned with black life on a deeper, more meaningful level."

*42 KLINKOWITZ, JEROME. "Black Superfiction." North American Review 259 (Winter):69-74.
    Cited in 1978.17.

43 KOSTELANETZ, RICHARD. The End of Intelligent Writing: Politics in America. New York: Sheed & Ward, pp. 239-40, 243, 308, 324, 346-47.
    19 Necromancers From Now is mentioned as an example of "superior though racially segregated anthologies." Yardbird Reader is "an exceptionally fine anthology."

44 LEHMANN-HAUPT, CHRISTOPHER. "Waiting for Solid Gumbo." New York Times, 21 October, p. 31.
    Points out that The Last Days of Louisiana Red is "a tangle of allusions and allegorical puzzles that keeps the mind on its toes. But once the puzzles are solved there isn't anything left over to feed our appetites. Unless of course we weren't very hungry to begin with. In which

case there isn't much point in devouring this novel at all."

45   No entry.

46   _____. "catechism of d neoamerican hoodoo church." In The Dark and Feeling: Black American Writers and Their Work. New York: Third Press, 53-54.
       Reprint of 1974.45.

*47   MEINKE, PETER. "La Poesia Norteamericana de hoy." Translated by Jorge Guitart. El Urogallo 27/28:22-27.
       Cited in 1978.48.

48   MERTZ, ROBERT JOSEPH. "Culture as Cataclysm: Disaster and Mass Values in Selected Contemporary American Fiction." Ph.D. dissertation, University of Minnesota.
       Explores one aspect of the imagination of disaster: the interrelationships between theories of mass society, criticism of mass culture, and selected works of fiction written since 1950. Reed's work is mentioned, with others, as suggesting that the destructive tendencies of mass society are inexorable.

49   MORRIS, JOE ALEX. "'Louisiana Red,' The Blight of America's Dream." Hartford (Conn.) Times, 1 December, p. 32.
       Brief discussion of the story of The Last Days of Louisiana Red. Morris states in part that "there is nothing standardized about the writing (blistering satire with nobody spared) or the plotting (zany secret agent mystery) or the characters (screwball good guys and bad guys and gals . . .)."

50   NEWTON, EDMUND. "Ishmael Reed." New York Post, 16 November, p. 33.
       Newton provides background biographical information in his review of Last Days of Louisiana Red including the facts that Reed once worked in a brassiere factory, was a reporter for The Newark Advance, and was a canvasser for the Daily News straw poll. Newton points out that Free-Lance Pallbearers grew out of an editorial Reed wrote for the Newark Weekly.

1974

51   NOLAN, TOM. "A Mix of Afro, Anglo, and Ho-ho." Los Angeles
      Times, 1 December, Calendar section, p. 70.
         Advances his opinion that The Last Days of Louisiana
      Red is a "wildly comic tale which moves with audacious
      alacrity from the punch of pulp fiction to the grim fam-
      iliarity of terrorist headlines to the mists of a voodoo
      Hades." Further, this is the "work of one of the most
      imaginative vital and enjoyable of American writers."

52   NORDELL, RODERICK. "Fiction." Christian Science Monitor,
      67, 18 December, p. 9.
         Offers a sketchy plot summary of Last Days of Louisiana
      Red.

53   RASPBERRY, WILLIAM. "Black Achievers." Washington Post,
      14 October, Section A, p. 29.
         Discussion of Reed's "Writer as Seer" (item IV.32) which
      observes, among other things, that "he is at his insight-
      ful, incisive best when he talks about the attacks (by
      black and white liberals) on black achievers."

54   RILEY, CAROLYN et al., eds. Contemporary Literary Criticism.
      Detroit, Mich.: Gale Research Co., Vol. 2, pp. 367-69.
         Cites "significant passages from the published criticism
      of work by well-known writers."

55   ROVIT, EARL. "Some Shapes in Recent American Fiction."
      Contemporary Literature 15:539-61.
         Surveys contemporary novels, 1970-1973, and includes
      comment on Mumbo Jumbo. Rovit concerns himself with de-
      fining the structures of what he sees as selling features,
      or not selling today and why.

56   SALE, ROGER. "Winter's Tales." New York Review of Books 21
      (12 December):18-22.
         Discusses The Last Days of Louisiana Red, along with
      other novels and finds Reed's fourth novel his best. Sale
      points out some of the technical shortcomings of the novel.

57   SCHMITZ, NEIL. "Down Home with Ishmael Reed: Chattanooga."
      Modern Poetry Studies (Autumn):205-7.
         Asserts of the title poem that "Reed is now approaching
      (not without hazard) some form of reconciliation with the
      American milieu in his writings." But of the whole,
      Schmitz finds "the achievement . . . as slender as the
      book itself."

1974

58 _____. "Neo-HooDoo: The Experimental Fiction of Ishmael Reed." Twentieth Century Literature 20 (April):126-40.
Explores the facets of Reed's writings up to and including Mumbo Jumbo and attempts to explicate Neo-HooDooism. Schmitz finds that Reed has yet to create a new focus for the Oral Tradition which he attempts to capture. But unlike others who have attempted similar things, Reed is fully aware of all the inherent difficulties. According to Schmitz, what distinguishes Reed from many others is Reed's "optimism, his belief that 'print and words are not dead at all' (19 Necromancers from Now, p. xxvii)." Excerpt reprinted in 1978.48, 1976.63.

59 SCHOLES, ROBERT. "The Last Days of Louisiana Red." New York Times Book Review, 10 November, p. 2.
Calls Ishmael Reed as important a satirist as Juvenal. However, beneath the satire "beats the heart of a preacher." Scholes believes that in this novel, Reed is exploring and attempting to tear down the myth of the matriarchal society (black society). Further, Scholes notes that the audience for this novel is Afro-American and that Reed is not directly concerned with the white middle class. Excerpt reprinted in 1976.63.

60 SHEPPARD, R. Z. "Gumbo Diplomacy." Time 104 (21 October): 114.
Tends toward synoptic plot summary of Last Days of Louisiana Red. There is a short biographical section at the end of the article. Excerpt reprinted in 1976.63.

61 SMITH, BARBARA. "Recent Fiction." New Republic 171 (23 November):53.
Finds The Last Days of Louisiana Red brilliant. But, "as a black woman, I am not nearly so enthusiastic." Excerpt reprinted in 1976.63 and 1978.48.

62 STUMPF, THOMAS. "Reviews." The Carolina Quarterly 26 (Winter):104.
Discusses Chattanooga as well as The Page Turner by David Shapiro, and No Vacancies by Daniel Epstein. Stumpf sums up the Reed section by noting "the chief emotion of Chattanooga is fierce, negligent joy, or the exuberant protean joy of Railroad Bill, the hero of Reed's best poem." Excerpt reprinted in 1976.63.

63 THOMAS, PHIL. "Prose Burns, Entertains." AP Newsfeatures, December, no pagination.
Reviews Last Days of Louisiana Red and offers little more than plot summary.

1974

64 _____. "Satiric look at Black life in America today." <u>San Francisco Chronicle</u>, 28 December, no pagination.
Points out that "Reed sees most clearly the many problems besetting contemporary society, describing them in a prose that burns while it entertains," in reviewing <u>The Last Days of Louisiana Red</u>.

65 VAUGHAN, KEVIN. "Louisiana Red." (University of Penn.) <u>Daily Pennsylvanian</u>, 7 November, p. 5.
Finds <u>The Last Days of Louisiana Red</u> Reed's best book to date. "The book contains a barb for everyone, hidden somewhere within the folds of Reed's colloquialism. <u>Louisiana Red</u> is thoroughly enjoyable reading material."

66 WARD, ED. "Some of the Most Useful and Diverting Tomes We Have Read Lately." <u>City</u> 7 (13 November–26 November):40-41.
Ward reviews <u>The Last Days of Louisiana Red</u>, recommending both Reed and the novel: "If you haven't yet discovered Ishmael Reed's powerful vision of black religion and culture or the crazy humor that he dishes out so generously, you're missing one of the best things the medium of print has to offer these days."

67 WASHBURN, MARTIN. "<u>Louisiana Red</u>." <u>Village Voice</u> 19 (November):41.
Mixed views on the novel. On the one hand Washburn points to it as "a very alive novel of living folklore; sometimes Reed's prose feels like walking through a field teeming with wild game which jump out from under your feet." On the other hand he says "it isn't easy to swallow the idea that any capitalist organization meets in heaven." Washburn compares <u>The Last Days of Louisiana Red</u> to T. S. Eliot's <u>The Cocktail Party</u>.

*68 WELBURN, RON. "Nationalism and Internationalism in Black Literature: The Afro-American Scene." <u>Greenfield Review</u> 3, no. 4:60-72.
Cited in 1978.48.

69 WOHLWEND, CHRIS. "It's that new black 'HooDoo.'" <u>The Charlotte</u> (N.C.) <u>Observer</u>, 10 November, no pagination.
Short comment on <u>The Last Days of Louisiana Red</u>. Wohlwend discovers that "Reed's subject is enhanced by an original writing style, a strange assortment of characters and knife-edged satire." The reviewer concludes saying Reed "brings a unique writing style to black literature and an ability to combine humor with his social commentary in a manner that is acerbic and effective."

70   YOUNG, AL. "Chattanooga." Changes (April):30.
        Asserts that Reed is "the most consistently interesting
     and original poet-novelist presently active on the North
     American continent." Young characterizes the poetry as
     "witty, melodic, mischievious, forever high-spirited and
     outrageous."

                            1975

*1   ABBOTT, RUTH, and SIMMONS, IRA. "Interview with Ishmael
        Reed." San Francisco Review of Books 1 (November):13-20.
           Cited in 1978.38.

*2   ANON. "Ellman, Reed will lecture in UB Literature Program."
        Buffalo Evening News, 23 June, p. 4.
           Cited in 1978.48.

  3   ANON. "Ishmael Reed Returning for U/B Modern Lit Event."
        Reporter, 15 May, p. 12.
           News article spotlights Reed's participation in the
        University of Buffalo's Summer Program in Modern Litera-
        ture. Extensive quotes are taken from the self-interview
        in Black World.

  4   ANON. "The Last Days of Louisiana Red." Book-of-the-Month
        Club News (February):27.
           Lists Louisiana Red as the month's alternate selection
        and quotes from a review of the novel published in
        Publishers Weekly.

  5   ANON. "The Last Days of Louisiana Red." The Erie (Penna.)
        Times-News, 26 January, p. 5-J.
           Calls the novel a "new display of verbal pyrotechnics."

  6   ANON. "Literary Notes." Philadelphia Inquirer, 24 January,
        no pagination.
           Shrovetide in Old New Orleans is mentioned briefly, in-
        cluding the comment that Reed is "often cited as the most
        gifted experimentalist among the black American writer."

  7   ANON. "Perspectives." Black World 24, no. 9 (July):59.
           Notes publication of Yardbird Reader vol. 3. Quotes
        Reed as calling it "America's only annual multi-cultural
        reader."

1975

8   ANON. "Reed, Ishmael. <u>The Last Days of Louisiana Red</u>."
<u>Choice</u> 12 (March):77-78.
    Notes that "Reed's parody on <u>Antigone</u> is worth the
price of the book."

9   ANON. "Reed, Ishmael." <u>A Directory of American Poets</u>. New
York: Poets & Writers, p. 23.
    Brief biographical listing.

10   ANON. "Reed, Ishmael." <u>Black American Writers Past and
Present: A Biographical and Bibliographical Dictionary</u>.
Edited by Theressa Rush et al. Metuchen, N.J.: Scarecrow
Press, Vol. 2, pp. 623-25.
    Routine biographic listing.

11   ANON. "The Ten Most Excellent Books." <u>City</u> 8 (8 January-
21 January):27.
    Lists <u>Last Days of Louisiana Red</u> as number one on the
list of the ten "most excellent books" of 1974.

12   ANON. "36 Prizes awarded in Arts and Letters: Pynchon Re-
jects His." <u>New York Times</u>, 22 May, p. 35.
    Announces a National Institute of Arts and Letters Award
which Reed won.

13   ANON. "UB to open 12th Summer Program." <u>Buffalo Courier-
Express</u>, 27 June, p. 9.
    Announces Reed's participation in University of
Buffalo's summer program.

14   ARMSTRONG, DAVID. "Literary Voodoo Magician Mixes Up Cure for
Reality." <u>Syracuse New Times</u>, 22 June, pp. 11-12.
    Far-reaching piece on Reed, his message, and his
methods, grouped around a review of <u>Last Days of Louisiana
Red</u>. "<u>Louisiana Red</u> has been accurately described as a
footnote to <u>Mumbo Jumbo</u>, but it is an extraordinarily rich
footnote that incorporates Reed's customary use of prophecy,
parody, time travel, astonishing quotations from arcane
works and mystical-religious asides in which he scatters
cultural reference points like a literary cropduster."

15   BAILEY, STEVE. "'Louisiana Red' Delightful but not Light-
Hearted Book." <u>Tallahassee</u> (Ga.) <u>Democrat</u>, 26 January,
p. 6E.
    Discusses <u>The Last Days of Louisiana Red</u> as a parallel
version of the Oedipus-Antigone myth. Bailey describes
the novel as "a delight. . . . The reader is rewarded on
almost every page by interesting use of words and keen
insights into social organization."

1975

16   BAKER, HOUSTON A. "The Last Days of Louisiana Red by Ishmael
      Reed." Black History Museum Umum Newsletter 4, no. 3-4:
      7-8.
          Finds the book to be a novel "Reed just had to get out
      of his system." Baker also finds that the novel relies too
      heavily on the formula of Mumbo Jumbo. For a fourth novel,
      Baker finds Louisiana Red just light reading.

17   _____ . "The Last Days of Louisiana Red." Black World 24
      (June):51-53.
          Portrays the novel as "sophomoric high-jinks. . . . much
      of its up-beat and on-the-spot philosophy is informed by
      what appears at times a sophomoric consciousness." Baker
      suggests that Reed "turn his sharp gaze back on the natural
      enemy behind--the one who built the papier-mâché . . . ."
      Of Reed's ability as a writer, Baker notes that he is one
      of the finest. Excerpt reprinted in 1976.63.

18   BANNON, ANTHONY. "Buffalo Premiere Proposed for Play on Local
      Novelist." Buffalo Evening News, 26 July, p. C8.
          News article.
          Follow-up news item: "Prize Winning Poem by UB Visiting
      Professor." Buffalo Evening News, 4 August, p. 9.

19   BETSKY, CELIA. "Low Profile: Ishmael Reed." Harper's Book-
      letter 1 (6 January):14.
          Short recounting of an interview with Reed. Reed makes
      further comments on his concept of hoodoo, and on his
      career and the creative life in California (even though he
      still considers New York to be the "center of more creativ-
      ity than any other place in the country"). The interview
      includes brief discussion on Last Days of Louisiana Red,
      Mumbo Jumbo, and Flight to Canada.

20   BONE, ROBERT. Down Home: A History of Afro-American Short
      Fiction from Its Beginnings to the End of The Harlem
      Renaissance. New York: G. P. Putnam's Sons, p. 75.
          Mentions Reed in a chapter on Charles Chesnutt.
      Chesnutt founded a satirical tradition which drew on the
      resources of the black folktale; this tradition descends
      through Langston Hughes and George Schuyler to William
      Melvin and Ishmael Reed.

21   CARTER, ALBERT HOWARD, III. "Three novels echo new generation
      of writers." St. Petersburg Times, 12 January, no pagina-
      tion.
          Compares and contrasts The Last Days of Louisiana Red
      with Guilty Pleasures by Donald Barthelme and Dog Soldiers

1975

by Robert Stone. Carter sees Reed's novel as "a mere
skeleton for [his] poetic versions of history, myth, and
social criticism." Carter believes the novel "will not
make a big splash, but will be admired and steadily con-
sumed by serious readers. . . . It will have imitators,
furthermore, so that Reed's technique will enter a wider
realm of American fiction, even down to the popular, com-
mercial writer."

22 COOPER, ARTHUR. "Call Him Ishmael." Newsweek 85 (2 June):75.
Cooper notes that Reed received the coveted Richard and
Hilda Rosenthal Foundation Award for his work in The Last
Days of Louisiana Red, and that Reed is "the most contro-
versial writer ever to receive a Rosenthal." Excerpt re-
printed in 1976.63.

23 DESRUISSEAUX, PAUL. "Ishmael Reed's Mumbo-Jumbo Literary
Gumbo." California Monthly 85 (June-July):1, 9.
A feature story about Reed's latest achievement with
Last Days of Louisiana Red and the winning of the Rosenthal
Foundation Award. The article discusses Reed's decision to
move from New York to Berkeley and his attempts at the
University of California at Berkeley to help his students
find their own literary voices.

24 FLEMING, ROBERT E. "Roots of the White Liberal Stereotype in
Black Fiction." Negro American Literature Forum 9:17-19.
Brief mention of Reed on page 19 which cites The Free-
Lance Pallbearers as an "all encompassing attack on
tokenism."

25 GARDNER, JOHN. "The Last Days of Louisiana Red." Jackson
(Tenn.) Sun, 5 January, no pagination.
Brief discussion and plot summary of the novel. Gardner
concludes that "mere plot summations, though, cannot begin
to do Reed's work justice. . . . This young caustic black
writer has not had his last say."

26 GAYLE, ADDISON, Jr. The Way of the New World: The Black
Novel in America. Garden City, N.Y.: Anchor Press/
Doubleday, pp. 135, 255, 273, 302, 309.
Reed is included in various places throughout this dis-
cussion of the development of black writing. Gayle says
that Reed is "perhaps the best black satirist since George
Schuyler."

27 JACKSON, LEANDRE. "Neo-Hoodooism: A Perspective." Black
History Museum Umum Newsletter 4, no. 3-4:3-6.
Jackson picks through Yellow Back Radio Broke-Down,
Mumbo Jumbo, "I am a Cowboy in the Boat of Ra," and The
Last Days of Louisiana Red to show how neo-hoodooism is a
reaction to contemporary misunderstanding of the black
aesthetic.

28 JAMES, CHARLES L. "Ishmael Reed." In Contemporary Poets.
Edited by James Vinson. New York: St. Martin's Press,
p. 1255.
Brief notice.

29 KENT, GEORGE E. "Notes on the 1974 Black Literary Scene."
Phylon 36 (June):182-203.
Reviewing the whole of the literary scene for 1974,
Kent takes The Last Days of Louisiana Red to task for not
having the freewheeling satire other of Reed's works have
shown. While Kent finds Reed's technical skills as a
writer good, on the whole he finds The Last Days of
Louisiana Red disappointing. The Reed portion of this
rather lengthy article is quite short. Excerpts reprinted
in 1978.48 and 1980.4.

30 KLINKOWITZ, JEROME. Literary Disruptions: The Making of a
Post-Contemporary American Fiction. Urbana: University
of Illinois Press, pp. 2, 176, 177, 182, 185-88.
Discusses Reed in various terms: "Ishmael Reed sees
himself as a modern American conjure man, whose new
aesthetic matches so closely the work of other American
disruptionists that his arguments against European deter-
minations (like LeRoi Jones's theories on the blues) apply
for all American, non-colonial work." The Free-Lance Pallbearers' narrative technique is called a "lyrical explora-
tion of a political exposé of Newark." Yellow Back Radio
Broke-Down, Mumbo Jumbo, 19 Necromancers From Now are also
discussed.

31 LEE, CHRISTOPHER HERRON. "A Gumbo of Black Humor: Voodoo and
a Red Rooster." Louisville (Ky.) Defender, 19 January, no
pagination.
Asserts that The Last Days of Louisiana Red is Reed's
weakest effort to date, "lacking in the looney overkill
humor that has been his novelistic trademark." Nevertheless, Lee states that Reed's books are "always structurally
intricate, full of obliquies and non-sequiturs" and concludes that this novel may be Reed's weakest, "but still
that puts it above most contemporary fiction."

1975

32 LINEBARGER, J. M., and ATKINSON, MONTE. "Getting to Whitey:
    Ishmael Reed's 'I am a Cowboy.'" <u>Contemporary Poetry: A
    Journal of Poetry Criticism</u> 2 (Spring):9-12.
        An explication of Reed's "I am a Cowboy in the Boat of
    Ra" which characterizes that poem as a "witty and compli-
    cated assault on white attitudes towards blacks," and notes
    the poem "argues that such white attitudes have frustrated
    blacks in their attempts at self-expression. . . . Reed
    manages to write his expressive poem in a highly original
    and forceful style."

33 LOCKE, HENRY D., Jr. "The Buffalo Homecoming of Writer/
    Publisher Ishmael Reed." <u>Buffalo Courier-Express Magazine</u>,
    31 August, no pagination.
        News story.

34 _____. "The Homecoming of Buffalo's Angry Young Man, Ishmael
    Reed." <u>Courier-Express Magazine</u>, 31 August, pp. 4-6.
        A news story covering Reed's return to Buffalo as a
    visiting professor at his alma mater, the University of
    Buffalo. Contains biographical details concerning Reed's
    early years in Buffalo.

35 LOVE, GLEN A. "Warren Miller: White Novelist in a Black
    World." <u>Negro American Literature Forum</u> 9:11-16.
        Mentions, on page 11, <u>The Free-Lance Pallbearers</u> and
    <u>Yellow Back Radio Broke-Down</u> in connection with author's
    search for good black American satire.

36 McCABE, CAROL. "A Good Hoodoo Man." <u>Providence</u> (R.I.) <u>Sunday
    Journal</u>, 15 January, p. H-28.
        Finds <u>The Last Days of Louisiana Red</u> to be "a wickedly
    funny novel written by a man whose blackness, credentials
    as an academician (at Berkeley) and youth permit him to
    take on a sackful of subjects others could not touch."
    Reed is called "one of the deepest young American
    novelists."

37 McFEE, MIKE. "Reed Explains Neo-HooDooism." <u>Daily Tar Heel</u>,
    5 February, p. 4.
        Reports on Reed as featured speaker at Fine Arts Fes-
    tival. Reed's Neo-HooDoo is described as "his urbane
    aesthetic, his philosophic art form, his master metaphor
    and his way of life." Reed on poets: "I don't like poets
    myself. A lot of them are crazy. There's probably more
    back-biting among poets than among politicians."

38 MacMILLAN, TERRY, and OUROUSSOFF, SANDRO. "Ishmael Reed:
    Poet, Publisher." Berkeley News, 10 April, p. 14. Re-
    printed in Black Times 5 (September):9-10.
        Reports an interview with Reed, in which he expounds his
    views regarding the state of American culture today, con-
    temporary black writers, and his own writing and publishing.

39 MONEY, MARY ALICE. "Evolutions of the Popular Western in
    Novels, Films, and Television, 1950-1974." Ph.D. disserta-
    tion, University of Texas at Austin.
        Yellow Back Radio Broke-Down is mentioned in this study
    of the popular Western as "Reed's Juvenalian satire."

40 MOSS, ROBERT F. "The Arts in Black America: Ishmael Reed,
    novelist." Saturday Review 3 (17 November):17.
        Notes in this general review of Reed's works, that
    Reed's poetry, "although sometimes entertaining, is too
    flippant to be taken seriously. His ready energy goes into
    his fiction." Moss asserts that Reed's predecessor is
    William Burroughs and that Reed has grafted Burroughs's
    techniques onto black culture. "Stylistically his work is
    lively. . . . theoretically and intellectually, however,
    he has boxed himself into much of the same
    other black writers have."

41 OAKS, PRISCILLA. "The Contemporary American Writer and His
    Sense of Ethnicity--or Is The Fishing Better in Your Own
    River?" MELUS 2 (December):2-3+.
        Spotlights the authors slated to appear at the 1975
    MELUS/MLA meeting at the San Francisco Hilton. Reed is
    heralded as "an unexpected but most welcome addition to our
    announced program."

42 O'BRIEN, JOHN THOMAS. "Interviews with Black Writers." Ph.D.
    dissertation, Northwestern Illinois University.
        See also 1973.33.

43 PFEIFFER, JOHN. "Black American Speculative Literature: A
    Checklist." Extrapolation 17 (December):35-43.
        Asserts that The Free-Lance Pallbearers is the "first of
    three critically acclaimed phantasmagoric fictions, combin-
    ing fable, myth, allegory and symbol--mock epic re-
    creations of America's most cherished institutions and
    myths." Article also mentions Yellow Back Radio Broke-Down
    and Mumbo Jumbo.

1975

*44   RIEGART, RAY. "Ishmael Reed Hoo-Doos the 'Cultural Nazis.'"
      Berkeley Barb, 12-18 December, no pagination.
            Cited in 1978.48.

 45   RILEY, CAROLYN et al., eds. Contemporary Literary Criticism.
      Vol. 3. Detroit, Mich.: Gale Research Co., pp. 424-25.
            Cites "significant passages from the published criticism
      of work by well-known writers."

 46   SCHMITZ, NEIL. "The Gumbo That Jes Grew." Partisan Review
      42:311-16.
            Notes that Reed made a shambles of the carefully articu-
      lated views of Ellison and Baldwin in his first novel, The
      Free-Lance Pallbearers, making it difficult for "those
      sympathetic critics who instinctively praise first novels
      of young black writers." Concerning The Last Days of
      Louisiana Red, Schmitz finds "there is a good deal of elu-
      sive action. . . . in fact the novel itself, for all its
      explosive topics, is ultimately evasive." Excerpt re-
      printed in 1976.63.

 47   THOMAS, PHIL. "Satiric Novel Views Black Life, Contemporary
      Problems." (Monterey, Penn.) Sunday Peninsula Herald,
      19 January, p. 8C.
            Brief review which consists mostly of plot highlights.
      "Reed takes the reader on a satiric tour of a fantasy
      land . . . that is not quite real, yet all too real. . . .
      Reed sees most clearly the many problems besetting con-
      temporary society, describing them in a prose that burns
      while it entertains."

 48   THOMAS, WILLIAM V. "Amos and Andy Revisited." Washington
      Star-News, 24 January, no pagination.
            Characterizes The Last Days of Louisiana Red as a work
      of "madcap genius that should establish Ishmael Reed as one
      of the best young comic writers in America."

 49   THOMPSON, M. CORDELL. "New York Beat." Jet Magazine
      (18 December):55.
            Notes on the New York scene. Concludes with this:
      "Critics who have read the script complain that Ragtime is
      a rip-off of Ismael [sic] Reed's Mumbo Jumbo, an off-beat
      account of how modern Black music developed in this
      country."

50   WARD, ED.   "The Last Days of Louisiana Red."   Creem (April):
         no pagination.
             One-sentence review; finds the novel to be "a sort of
         extended footnote to his Mumbo Jumbo."

51   YOUNG, AL.   "Fiction: Introduction."   Iowa Review 6, no. 2
         (Spring):42–44.
             Consists of introductory remarks about four young black
         writers whose works appear elsewhere in the issue.   Reed
         is depicted as "a dauntless iconoclast and a scholarly
         Americana enthusiast, . . . this country's most original
         young literary stylist, a satirist who does not hesitate to
         assail hypocrisy and social injustice wherever he uncovers
         it."   Young asserts that Reed's "hilarious barbs are meant
         to expose human folly, mendacity, absurdity and wickedness
         with an eye to tempering their evil effects."

                            1976

1   ABBOTT, RUTH.   "San Francisco Review of Books: Flight to
         Canada."   San Francisco 2, no. 7 (November):24.
             Abbott reviews Flight to Canada, finding it funny and
         taking leave of traditional Aristotelian poetics.   However,
         she finds the novel both entertaining and informative:
         "two criteria I believe Aristotle himself set down for good
         literature."

2   ANON.   "Books."   Playboy 23 (October):30, 32.
             A brief notice that says of Flight to Canada, "it's
         about 194 pages of sheer pleasure, but don't ask what it
         adds up to."   The reviewer sums: "Put it this way:
         Ragtime is the literary version of history.   Roots is the
         current journalistic version of history.   And Flight to
         Canada is the rock-'n'-roll version of history."

3   ANON.   "Books Briefly Noted: Flight to Canada."   New Yorker
         52 (22 November):210.
             Finds Flight to Canada "merely exhausting" despite the
         fact that all Reed's novels have "sardonic fantasy, fast,
         bitter dialogue, and complex insights into various aspects
         of black culture."

4   ANON.   "Fiction."   Boston Phoenix, 9 November, p. 8.
             Calls Flight to Canada "a riotous conflation of his-
         torical and literary tidbits, trash-talking and highbrow
         cant" but finds that it "comes dangerously close at times
         to renouncing life in the name of the language with which
         its author plays."

1976

5   ANON. "Flight to Canada." Kirkus Reviews 44 (15 July):810.
        The reviewer notes that "Reed is an expert stylist with
      a fine sense of timing; here he fuses history, fantasy,
      political reality with ragtimed syncopation. Cryptic and
      chaotic, this has a sassy swagger as well as its own inner
      logic."

6   ANON. "Flight to Canada by Ishmael Reed." Cultural Informa-
      tion Service (October):19.
        Finds the novel an "attempt to imaginatively exorcise
      all the demons from black consciousness." Also, the re-
      viewer finds that Reed's use of an outrageous story line
      serves to "make some searing observations on blacks who
      sell out their souls thinking they are getting freedom."

7   ANON. "Read all about it." Black Times (May):14.
        Notice of publication of Conjure--consists of a two-
      paragraph quotation from the foreword.

8   ANON. "Reed, Ishmael." Contemporary Poets. Edited by James
      Vinson. 2nd ed. New York: St. Martin's Press,
      pp. 1153-54.
        Biographical listing.

9   ANON. "Reed, Ishmael." A Directory of American Fiction
      Writers. New York: Poets & Writers, p. 23.
        Brief biographical listing.

10   BANNON, BARBARA. "PW Forecasts: Fiction." Publishers Weekly
      210 (9 August):67.
        Notice of Flight to Canada asserting "Reed's new novel
      is a fantasy, an experiment, a trip and it's not going to
      be to anybody's liking. Reed obviously is into an allegory
      of sorts and on some level it is successful."

11   BATCHELOR, JOHN CALVIN. "Ishmael Reed Raises Questions About
      Abe Lincoln's Identity." Soho Weekly News, 14 October,
      p. 19+.
        Reports interview with Reed in which they discuss Flight
      to Canada, among other things. The conversation touches on
      the Ragtime/Mumbo Jumbo controversy: "I ain't sayin' he
      stole it, but Doctorow was in the audience one night at a
      reading I gave for Mumbo Jumbo. I guess you could say I
      gave it away. And my technique was genuine ragtime."
      Batchelor also states that Reed is "already assured of
      going down as one of the great American novelists of the
      mid-twentieth century" and that "his books are constantly
      threatening to break into song."

12 BELL, GENE H. "Fantasy, History and the New Fiction."
      Commonweal 103, no. 23 (5 November):718-23.
         In this study of how contemporary writers have used
      historical models and how these models have been accepted,
      Bell finds Reed's work, Mumbo Jumbo, to be one of several
      major works. It is an "intellectually energetic and vi-
      sionary" work "that just misses being perfect."

13 BELLAMY, JOE DAVID. "Books in Brief: Flight to Canada."
      Saturday Review 4 (2 October):35.
         Comments "Reed deliberately mixes fact and fiction,
      hilarious anachronisms, folklore, and personal mythology,
      caricature and idiom, all for choice comic effect. . . . It
      is a world skillfully designed to allow the free play of a
      talent for hyperbole and downright yarning unequaled since
      Twain and for the impressive energy and stunning improvisa-
      tions of an original and exciting comic imagination."

14 _____. "Ishmael Reed, Flight to Canada." Fiction Inter-
      national 6/7:148-49.
         Finds Flight to Canada to be zany, witty, and comic, a
      comedy which comes from the pages of history but more
      "straight from the fevered absurdist imagination of its
      author."

15 BENSON, BRIAN. "A Trio of Slaves in Flight, in Jest."
      Greensboro (N.C.) Daily News, 17 October, no pagination.
         Benson finds Flight to Canada shows signs of brilliance.
      He notes that the other Reed novels were "good solid
      novels."

16 BERGMANN, LINDA S. "Flight to Canada." Chicago Review 28
      (Fall):200-205.
         Compares Reed with Roth, Doctorow, Pynchon, and Barth
      as authors who have "renewed and transformed the once be-
      littled historical novel." Flight to Canada is viewed as
      having destroyed the stereotype of so many historical
      novels. Bergmann concludes that "the brilliance of Reed's
      work rests in his translation of a new interpretation of
      our past into a new form of historical novel."

17 BERMAN, HAROLD. "Letters: Much Ado About Voodoo."
      Washington Post, 5 September, Section G, p. 10.
         Letter in response to Reed's review of The Treasury of
      Afro-American Folklore by Harold Courlander (see IV.42).
      Berman faults Reed for having more to say about himself
      and his own erudition than about the book under considera-
      tion. "A knowledgeable, thoughtful and intelligent review

1976

of a serious book is an important service to both writers
and readers. By the same token, one that is not is a dis-
tinct disservice."

18   BIGELOW, BRUCE. "Ishmael Reed Spices Language With 'Gumbo.'"
     (Berkeley) <u>Daily Californian</u>, 3 March, p. 3.
        Short overview of Reed's literary career to date.
     Quotes Reed as saying that contrary to some critics' alle-
     gations, his early influence was not William Burroughs, but
     rather Nathanael West.

19   BRUNSKILL, JOAN. "Novel Will Please Good Literature Fans."
     <u>Asheville Citizen-Times</u>, 17 October, p. 21C.
        <u>Flight to Canada</u> is discussed. "Let all good gray his-
     torians take warning. This is a book that could mightily
     offend their sense of professional propriety--unless they
     have a taste for good literature and a sense of humor, in
     which case they will be mightily entertained and perhaps
     even provoked to revisionism."

20   CAMPENNI, FRANK. "Up From Slavery In a New Recipe."
     <u>Milwaukee Journal</u>, 17 October, no pagination.
        Campenni looks at the novels of Reed (<u>Flight to Canada</u>);
     Haley (<u>Roots</u>); Williams (<u>Captain Blackman</u>, <u>The Autobiog-
     raphy of Miss Jane Pittman</u>); and Ellison (<u>Invisible Man</u>),
     to discover the connections that each author uses to bring
     fact into the fictional world. Only Reed blends past and
     present "with his time-splattering mixmaster serving up a
     devil's food cake spiced with almonds of anecdote, anach-
     ronism and epigram."

21   CARTER, STEVEN R. "Ishmael Reed's NeoHooDoo Detection." In
     <u>Dimensions of Detective Fiction</u>. Edited by Larry Landrum,
     Pat Browne, and Ray B. Browne. Bowling Green State Univer-
     sity, Ohio: Popular Press, pp. 265-90.
        Lengthy discussion of <u>Mumbo Jumbo</u> as detective fiction.
     Carter characterizes Reed as regarding "the mystery novel
     as a vehicle for getting at other mysteries, such as the
     'mysteries of the American civilization,' which he wishes
     to de-mystify." Carter discusses <u>The Last Days of
     Louisiana Red</u> as a straight crime novel, "close, but not
     quite."

22   _____. "Ishmael Reed's NeoHooDoo Detection." <u>Proceedings of
     the 6th National Convention of the Popular Culture Associa-
     tion, April 22-24, 1976</u>. Edited by Michael T. Marsden.
     Bowling Green State University, Ohio: Popular Press,
     pp. 186-210.
        Reprint of 1976.21.

1976

23 CHARYN, JEROME. "Flight to Canada." New York Times Book
       Review, 19 September, pp. 5, 12.
           Depicts the novel as "a demonized 'Uncle Tom's Cabin,'
       [sic] a book that reinvents the particulars of slavery in
       America with a comic rage. . . . Time becomes a modest,
       crazy fluid in Reed's head, allowing him to mingle events
       of the last 150 years, in order to work this magic."
       Charyn concludes that Flight to Canada is "a hellish book
       with its own politics and a muscular, luminous prose. It
       should survive."

24 COLLINS, TERENCE GEORGE. "A Psychoanalytic Introduction To
       Reader Response to Racial Literature." Ph.D. dissertation,
       University of Minnesota.
           Defines and illustrates ways in which the anxiety of
       separation and the fantasy of dirt play a key role in
       shaping the response of readers to texts loosely defined
       as "racial." Poetry of the black arts movement is de-
       scribed as affirming the political need for a new soli-
       darity. Reed, Baraka, Lee (Don) are briefly discussed.

25 COURLANDER, HAROLD. "Letters: Much Ado About VooDoo."
       Washington Post, 5 September, Section G, p. 10.
           Letter in response to Reed's review of Treasury of Afro-
       American Folklore by Harold Courlander (See IV.42).
       Courlander takes exception to Reed's evaluation in general,
       and specifically to the assessment of the passages on Haiti
       and Vodoun. "Isn't a reviewer supposed to get at least
       acquainted with the main body of the book he is reviewing?"

26 EDWARDS, THOMAS R. "Books in Brief: Five Novels." Harper's
       Magazine 253 (October):100-101.
           Comments briefly on Flight to Canada: "Continuously
       funny and provocative, but it lacks the imaginative alchemy
       that made Reed's Mumbo Jumbo such an exhilarating anti-
       history."

27 EVANS, JAMES. "Novelist Ishmael Reed Puts Heavy Demands on
       Reader." (Monterey, Penn.) Sunday Peninsula Herald,
       3 October, p. 120.
           Evans sums Reed's dilemma in a discussion of Flight to
       Canada: "He is harangued by the left for being too con-
       servative, and denounced by the right as too radical, and
       is practically unknown by the middle." The novel is "a
       highly intelligent and entertaining work."

1976

28   FABRE, MICHEL. "Ishmael Reed: The Free-Lance Pallbearers ou
     le langage au pouvoir." Revue Française d'Etudes Ameri-
     caines 1, no. 1:83-100.
          Takes up a lengthy and detailed discussion of the lan-
     guage in Free-Lance Pallbearers. Through his analysis of
     style, form, and genre, Fabre concludes: "Having ques-
     tioned the function of language in a repressive socio-
     political system through the metaphor of shit, he [Reed]
     sets up the dynamics of linguistic performance as a viable
     alternative." Throughout his study, Fabre points to the
     qualities of action vs. stasis and notes that Reed rebels
     against stasis. In French.

29   FERRALL, TALISHIAN. "A Splendid Offering From a Writer with
     Style and Wit." New York Amsterdam News, 4 December,
     p. D-3.
          Enthusiastic discussion of Flight to Canada. Ferrall
     states that "every now and then one happens upon a writer
     who has the wit, style and intelligence to kindle the fires
     in a threadbare subject and creates a work that explodes.
     Ishmael Reed is such a man and Flight to Canada is such a
     work." The reviewer sums it up, saying "Reed is expressing
     a sense of anger and bewilderment at the sameness of the
     past, present and future abuses heaped on the Black man by
     others and himself."

30   FIRESTONE, BRUCE M. "Flight to Canada." Library Journal 101
     (August):1659.
          Characterizes Flight to Canada as "a rich mordant,
     funny, very wise novel . . . a first rate work: proof that
     Ishmael Reed, novelist, poet, and voodoo man, has emerged
     as a major and distinctive voice in American writing."

31   FLEMING, ROBERT. "Creative, Unique, Personal View."
     Freedomways 16, no. 4:257-58.
          Reviews Flight to Canada, finding it full of sight gags,
     humor which brings with it more than surface observation.
     The book is "well researched. It is worthy of your
     attention."

32   FLOWERS, CHARLES. "Joyfully Erudite Look at America."
     Chattanooga News, 10 October, no pagination.
          Flight to Canada is "the novel Ragtime was thought to
     be." Flowers, in comparing Reed with Doctorow, finds
     Doctorow sententious while "Reed skips lightly by firing
     in unpredictable and brilliantly loony directions." The
     construction of the novel leaves the reader "afloat on a

sea of puns, metaphors, and historical games that could, in lesser hands, have become a tsunami of cuteness and other kinds of excess."

33   FOOTE, BUD. "Fleeing Uncle Tom's Mansion by 747." <u>National Observer</u> 15 (9 October):24.
      Says that Reed has once again stirred up past, present, real, and fantastic into a crazy gumbo in <u>Flight to Canada</u>: "If you are with me in enjoying this sort of foolishness, and if you find the use of anachronism humorous and mind-expanding, no doubt you have already discovered Ishmael Reed. . . . If not, then you probably wouldn't like him anyway, and you may be just too totally sane to survive in this goofy world."

34   FOX, ROBERT ELLIOT. "The Mirrors of Caliban: A Study of the Fiction of Leroi Jones (Imamu Amiri Baraka), Ishmael Reed and Samuel Delany." Ph.D. dissertation, State University of New York at Buffalo.
      In an attempt to trace the development of the imaginary visions of three major authors and to trace their individual developments in the various fictive forms, Fox cites Ishmael Reed, among others, as a key element in developing a black aesthetic. Fox treats <u>The Free-Lance Pallbearers</u>, <u>Yellow Back Radio Broke-Down</u>, <u>Mumbo Jumbo</u>, <u>The Last Days of Louisiana Red</u>, and a shorter piece "Cab Calloway Stands In For the Moon; or, D Hexorcism of Noxon D Awful," and says that Reed is close to Leroi Jones in Reed's "The Gangster's Death," "The Ghost in Birmingham," and "The Jackal-Headed Cowboy." Fox mentions Reed's acknowledgment of influences by West's <u>The Dream Life of Balso Snell</u>, Kenneth Patchen's <u>The Journal of Albion Moonlight</u>, and Charles Wright's <u>The Wig</u>, as well as the influence of the German Expressionist film, <u>The Cabinet of Dr. Caligary</u>. Perhaps the clearest summary of Fox's discussion of Reed is that "for him [Reed] there are many realities behind the jealously guarded gates of singularity, the somber edifice of official Reality."

35   GALDONIK, MICHEL. "Reviews in Brief." <u>Charleston</u> (W. Va.) <u>Evening Post</u>, 24 October, no pagination.
      In a very brief review of <u>Flight to Canada</u>, Wilson finds it "a splendid comedy, it has bearing on America's past and present and is particularly aimed at an everpresent in-equity--racism."

1976

36   GAYLE, ADDISON, Jr. "Black Women and Black Men: The Litera-
         ture of Cartharsis." <u>Black Books Bulletin</u> 4 (Winter):48-52.
            Criticizes Reed and Gayle Jones for typifying in their
         respective novels--<u>Flight to Canada</u> and <u>Eva's Man</u>--a war of
         the sexes. Gayle would prefer artists to take responsi-
         bility by pointing out the "truths" of racism in America:
         poverty, unemployment, and child mortality.

37   _____. "Ishmael Reed." In <u>Contemporary Novelists</u>. Edited by
         James Vinson. New York: St. Martin's Press, pp. 1153-54.
            Brief notice.

38   GRAY, PAUL. "Yoknapatawpha Blues." <u>Time</u> 108 (27 September):
         92-93.
            <u>Flight to Canada</u> gets one paragraph (on page 93) of this
         article, the thesis of which is that Southern writing seems
         "stalled between the glorious past and an uncertain future."
         Reed's section concludes: "The target of Reed's broad,
         sometimes raging satire is American racism. But the South
         is also, in its readymade exaggerations, the best friend
         his fiction has."

39   HOGAN, WILLIAM. "Mumbo Jumbo." <u>San Francisco Chronicle</u>,
         20 September, p. 53.
            Finds <u>Flight to Canada</u> a "comic novel, and while it may
         not be everyone's cup of mint julep, it does capture the
         world of high comic style."

40   HUNTER, KRISTIN. "The High Priest of Neo-HooDoo." <u>Phila-
         delphia Sunday Bulletin</u>, 10 October, no pagination.
            While Hunter praises <u>Flight to Canada</u>, she finds it not
         up to the level of <u>Mumbo Jumbo</u>. Quicksill, the slave who
         "describes the author's talent--the quick skill with which
         he turns out prose like an action painter producing a can-
         vas, slapping on horror, humor, history and fantasy in
         large bright daubs."

41   IVIE, ARDIE. "Anachronistic Antagonisms." <u>Los Angeles Times</u>,
         5 November, Section 4, p. 30.
            Asserts that <u>Flight to Canada</u> like all Reed's previous
         novels, is "written in an allegorical and, at times, poetic
         style. There is deliberate integration of prose and
         poetry which Reed considers to be a revolt against cul-
         tural slavery and the customary boundaries that exist be-
         tween the two forms of literature. . . . it moves . . .
         like magic."

42   JEFFERSON, MARGO. "Black Mischief." <u>Newsweek</u> 88 (20 December):96.
        Jefferson notes <u>Flight to Canada</u> is a "staccato-paced satire on the varieties of slavery--physical, verbal, emotional--the deceptive guises of freedom, and the cultural politics involved in writing about the black experience."

43   KLINKOWITZ, JEROME. "Reed's Slapstick History." <u>Chicago Daily News Panorama</u>, 25-26 September, p. 11.
        Reviews <u>Flight to Canada</u>, finding it the best of Reed's novels to date. Klinkowitz portrays the novel as an anachronism in the best sense, slapstick comedy, and praises the Reed Voo-Doo charms: "Reed has proven himself again as a writer who can compete with any other contemporary cultural medium--and win again."

44   LANDRY, DONNA. "Incantation and Parody." <u>Washington Post</u>, 12 October, p. 86.
        A news item about Reed's appearance at the nineteenth reading of the Ascension Poetry Series held at the Folger Shakespeare Library and his reading of selections from <u>Flight to Canada</u>. Also appearing on the same program was Jayne Cortez. Landry sums up the evening: "In all, it was a two-hour exchange at the Folger in which one was not read to; one laughed and survived."

45   LeCLAIR, THOMAS. "A Mixture of Flavors." <u>Cincinnati Inquirer</u>, 12 September, no pagination.
        LeClair laments the fact that <u>Flight to Canada</u> will be compared to Doctorow's <u>Ragtime</u> when <u>Mumbo Jumbo</u> should have been. Further, LeClair finds the comparison unfortunate because <u>Flight to Canada</u> "doesn't have the force or wit of Reed's four other novels--original, imaginative books that give Reed the eminence Ellison and Baldwin had ten years ago."

46   McCLELLAND, DON. "Four Yardbirds: The Guest Word." <u>New York Times Book Review</u>, 1 February, p. 35.
        Recounts the history of the <u>Yardbird Readers</u>: "It's a very healthy journey for any color of imagination to visit the other countries of the mind that the <u>Yardbird</u> series showcases in its ethnic spectrum. There's a lot of fetish-making and breaking, conjuring, talkin' [sic] trash, signifying, prophesying, doing that thing." Discusses <u>Yardbird Reader</u> Volume Four in more detail.

1976

47 _____. "Four Yardbirds: The Guest Word." Yardbird Reader.
   Vol. 5, p. 322.
      Reprint of 1976.46.

48 McINTYRE, SOLOMON. "Black Scribes Call for More Black Publishers." Atlanta Voice, 15 May, no pagination.
      McIntyre reports the discussion at the Second Annual
   National Conference of Afro-American Writers. At that
   conference Addison Gayle denounced Reed's Last Days of
   Louisiana Red because it was "negative in scope" and did
   little to enhance an "already negative view that Blacks
   take in some cases toward one another."

49 McKENZIE, JAMES. "Pole Vaulting in Top Hats: a Public Conversation with John Barth, William Gass, and Ishmael Reed."
   Modern Fiction Studies 22 (Summer):131-51.
      Reed discusses and comments on the origins and develop-
   ment of Mumbo Jumbo and Free-Lance Pallbearers. He also
   mentions Flight to Canada and Yellow Back Radio Broke-Down.
   He also makes reference to the existence of literary politics and states his belief that "there's a cultural Water-
   gate that hasn't been exposed yet."

50 MacNAMEE, MAX. "Raucous Voice." Hartford Courant,
   17 October, no pagination.
      Flight to Canada is "not your average fugitive slave
   novel." Reed is "clearly one of our finest and most important novelists." MacNamee believes "Reed writes like a
   happy barbarian and succeeds in bringing history down to
   our present-day level."

*51 MAJOR, CLARENCE. "Tradition and Presence: Experimental Fic-
   tion by Black American Writers." American Poetry Review 5
   (May/June):33-34.
      Cited in 1978.17.

52 MARCUS, GREIL. "Uncle Tom Redux." Village Voice 21, no. 46
   (15 November):47, 49.
      Reviews Flight to Canada, offering that it is Reed's bid
   to retake the Uncle Tom story away from Harriet Beecher
   Stowe because it is probably "too valuable to leave to a
   white writer." Of Reed in general, Marcus concludes that
   he is one of the most "ambitious writers black or white."

53 MILLER, ALICIA METCALF. "Fugitive Slave's Flight--A Time-warp
    Exercise in Fantasy." <u>Cleveland Plain Dealer</u>, 24 October,
    sect. 6, p. 8.
         Miller finds <u>Flight to Canada</u> "great fun, but ultimately,
    the sum of the novel is not as great as its parts." She
    discusses the novel in terms of going one step further than
    Doctorow by fooling around with chronology as well as with
    historical characters.

54 NORDELL, RODERICK. "The Civil War . . . in 'stereo.'"
    <u>Minneapolis Tribune</u>, 31 October, no pagination.
         Reprint of 1976.55.

55 _____. "Where History Happens All At Once." <u>Christian
    Science Monitor</u>, 20 October, p. 25.
         A substantial though short discussion of Reed's novel
    <u>Flight to Canada</u> and his technique. Nordell asserts that
    this latest book should "add to his reputation as one of
    America's most freshly--and bizarrely--imaginative sati-
    rists," and that he was playing with characters in history
    before Doctorow "brought best seller attention to the
    technique." The review characterizes Reed as ranging from
    "intellectual subtlety to the depths of degradation in
    symbolically linking self-enslavement to the impulse to
    enslave others." Excerpts reprinted in 1978.48.

56 O'CONNELL, SHAUN. "American Fiction, 1975: Celebration in
    Wonderland." <u>Massachusetts Review</u> 17, no. 1 (Spring):
    165-94.
         Lengthy discussion of outstanding fiction of 1975.
    Reed's <u>The Last Days of Louisiana Red</u> (p. 175) is a "whacko
    allegory of sorts" that succeeds in no small part due to
    the fact that "Reed has as much talent as any living
    novelist."

57 _____. "The Vitality of Black Life." <u>Boston Globe</u>,
    14 November, no pagination.
         Brief notice: "While the plot of <u>Flight to Canada</u>
    celebrates the vitality of black life, what finally emerges
    for celebration is the vital life of the novel itself in
    Reed's joyous hands."

58 PAUL, BARBARA. "'Canada' A Satire of America." <u>Pittsburgh
    Press</u>, 19 September, no pagination.
         Paul praises <u>Flight to Canada</u> because "the humor is
    always upbeat, never bitter. It is refreshing to read a
    writer so comfortable with himself."

1976

58a PETRIE, PHIL W. "<u>Flight to Canada</u>." <u>Encore American and
        Worldwide News</u>, 18 October, p. 44.
            Discussion of Reed's fifth novel. "If you enjoyed [the
        previous four novels], then you'll enjoy <u>Flight to Canada</u>.
        Each novel, of course, is different from the other but, in
        the vernacular of some Blacks, it's the same difference."
        Petrie also draws the parallel between <u>Flight</u> and <u>Ragtime</u>:
        "Some may even suggest--if they consider themselves to be
        kind--that Reed is a Black Doctorow. (Although when one
        considers Reed's four previous novels one wonders why this
        characterization shouldn't be in the reverse.)"

59   PLEASANTS, BEN. "<u>Yardbird Reader Volume 4</u>." <u>Bookswest</u> 1,
        no. 3 (November/December):45.
            Finds that the volume "helps turn back the racist myth
        expressed by critics like Leslie Fiedler that blacks are
        without a culture or a history."

60   RAMELLA, RICHARD. "Bookshelf: Ishmael Reed's Newest."
        <u>Independent Journal and Gazette</u>, 21 September, no pagina-
        tion.
            Recommends <u>Flight to Canada</u> because "Reed continues to
        be an excellent wordsmith. And . . . he shows himself
        again capable of commenting on contemporary matters within
        an entertaining and humorous framework."

61   REDMOND, EUGENE. <u>Drumvoices: The Mission of Afro-American
        Poetry--A Critical History</u>. Garden City, N.Y.: Anchor
        Press, pp. 11, 32-33, 131, 298, 308, 311, 312, 318-19,
        348, 349, 406-8, 410.
            Brief mentions throughout the book. Reed is innovative
        in his "use of supernatural themes, characters and
        vocabulary."

62   RHODES, RICHARD. "Reed's Merger of Past and Present."
        <u>Chicago Tribune</u>, 3 October, Section 7, pp. 2, 6.
            Enthusiastic review. Reed "takes on Civil War America
        and shrivels it to its irrational roots in 179 coruscating
        pages of, literally, black humor. The method is not sur-
        realism; it is rather the comic puncturing of fact to
        bleed it of its otherwise invisible humors: the method of
        the essay grafted to the madness of comic fiction." Gen-
        erally finds <u>Flight to Canada</u> to be worthwhile reading.

63 RILEY, CAROLYN et al., eds. Contemporary Literary Criticism.
    Vol. 6. Detroit, Mich.: Gale Research, pp. 447-50.
        Cites "significant passages from the published criticism
    of work by well-inown writers."

64 ROSENBLATT, ROGER. "North Toward Home." Washington Post,
    14 November, Section L, p. 4.
        Says that the trouble with Flight to Canada is that
    "too many of Reed's jokes are weak or old standup routines,
    and when you have come to the end of his joy ride you
    haven't laughed enough to be moved by the change of direc-
    tion. Comedy has to laugh at something other than itself
    to bring down the house. Or to build it up again."

65 SABATINI, ARTHUR J. "His Own Wild Version of History."
    Philadelphia Inquirer, 26 September, no pagination.
        Finds Flight to Canada as much a funhouse as Reed's
    other novels. Sabatini says "the language and humor . . .
    sometimes get too slippery and elliptical but . . . in its
    own way comes together in another satisfying Reed."

66 SIMON, JEFF. "Buffalo the Setting of a Wild Novel." Buffalo
    Evening News, 2 October, p. C-12.
        Reviewing Flight to Canada, Simon points out that "the
    difficulty with Reed's 'anything goes' revisionism about
    slavery, American literature and the Civil War is that his
    modes clash badly at times." On the whole Simon asserts
    that Reed's "reckless darting comedies make surprising
    sense."

67 SIMON, MYRON. "Two Angry Ethnic Writers." MELUS 3, no. 2:
    pp. 20-24.
        Reply to Reed's "Crushing the Mutiny" (IV.39).

68 TAYLOR, CLYDE. "Garvey's Ghost: Revamping the Twenties."
    Black World 25 (February):54-67.
        Gives an historical review of a number of recent and
    not-so-recent publications which center on the Harlem
    Renaissance, but includes Reed's Mumbo Jumbo. He finds
    Reed's work worth reading but takes it to task for por-
    traying the Renaissance as a "happy place" and ignoring
    what Taylor believes to be the major battle: Garveyism.

69 THOMAS, LORENZO. "Two Crowns of Thoth: A Study of Ishmael
    Reed's The Last Days of Louisiana Red." Obsidian 2, no. 3:
    pp. 5-25.
        Thomas's study of Last Days of Louisiana Red rambles
    almost incoherently from subject to subject with very

1976

little unification, clarity of purpose, or point of view.
It is filled with statements such as "Silly if one is trying to make a masterpiece, but you damn bet you serious if
you trying to make groceries." Or "If there is anything
of convention here, it is the fantastic apparitional con-
tinuity of the modern motion picture . . . Hold it. All of
that is fodder for formalists." While this study examines
in some detail the psychic qualities of red and the qualities of the past, Thomas finds on the whole that Louisiana
Red is both too consciously a "written novel" (as opposed
to Reed's desire to be a story teller) and "automatic
writing at its best." Mr. Thomas does offer one interesting anecdote concerning Louisiana Red—that the manufac-
turers of Tabasco sauce tried to hold up its publication
because they thought Reed was trying to put them out of
business.

70   TURNER, DARWIN. "A Spectrum of Blackness." Parnassus:
     Poetry in Review 4, no. 2 (Spring/Summer):202-19.
        Compares the style and techniques of Reed and Alice
     Walker in a review of Conjure and Chattanooga and Walker's
     Revolutionary Petunias and Other Poems. He finds Reed's
     works to be in the mainstream of traditional black poetic
     subject matter. But unlike other poets Reed poses diffi-
     culty in categorizing all thematic concerns. Turner notes
     that Reed doesn't organize his works around central the-
     matic concerns but rather allows them to flow from present
     to past as a turn on a roulette wheel. Turner does note
     that Henderson's analysis of black poetry in Understanding
     The New Black Poetry (1973) is followed point by point by
     Reed in these two books of poetry. Excerpts reprinted in
     1980.4.

71   TURNER, JOSEPH WILLIAM. "The Comic Historical Novel: Some
     Recent Experiments." Ph.D. dissertation, Emory University.
        Turner discusses Yellow Back Radio in great detail and
     gives substantial consideration to the place of the his-
     torical novel and its conventions. He finds that the non-
     traditional historical novel presents untold problems for
     literary critics. Of Yellow Back Radio, which he classi-
     fies as an hybrid historical novel, Turner notes that in
     parts, its charm is the multi-dimensionality of plot. Reed
     is for Turner more elusive than T. S. Eliot. The discus-
     sion also includes Barth's Sot Weed Factor and Thomas
     Berger's Little Big Man.

1977

72   TYLER, RALPH. "Literary Figures Offer Plots and Quips." <u>New York Times</u>, 1 August, Section II, pp. 1, 13+.
        Reed joins with other writers such as Updike, Dickey, and Asimov in advancing brief recommendations for a sequel to <u>Gone With The Wind</u>.

73   WEBSTER, IVAN. "Plantation Pranks." <u>Newsday</u>, 3 October, no pagination.
        Webster's review of <u>Flight to Canada</u> warns readers that they "must become agile, willing respecters of time warps." And of Reed, Webster notes his "raillery has never had quite such unrelenting, double-edged clutch and bite."

74   WHITE, EDMUND. "A Fantasia on Black Suffering." <u>The Nation</u> 223, no. 8 (18 September):247-49.
        <u>Flight to Canada</u> is the subject of White's review. He considers Reed the "best black writer around," and compares the characterization in Reed's latest novel to Balzac's, noting that Balzac's writing pointed out the genius of each of his characters, much the way Reed does.

75   WICKSTROM, ANDY. "History on the Wing." <u>Virginian Pilot</u>, 1 September, no pagination.
        Wickstrom finds <u>Flight to Canada</u> has "some astute things to say about racism and its part in the makeup of the American character, but the author's unorthodox ways dilute the force of his message."

76   WINOKUR, SCOTT. "He's Licked the Slave Mentality." <u>Oakland Tribune</u>, 19 October, no pagination.
        Finds <u>Flight to Canada</u> "a satire and an utterly wild inversion of everything you thought you knew about the Civil War." He also reports a loosely-structured interview with Reed in which he talks about his life and work.

<u>1977</u>

1   ALLEN, BRUCE. "Black Slaves and Arctic Balloons." <u>Baltimore Sun</u>, 16 January, no pagination.
        Finds <u>Flight to Canada</u> provocative and fun. Allen also indicates that a casual reader might find the novel silly. But on the whole, he says that Reed is "doing a number on us all . . . [it's] a hell of a lot more than the sum of its parts, and it will get you, if you don't watch out."

1977

2   ANON. "Books: Recent Books Received." <u>First World: An
     International Journal of Black Thought</u> 1 (January/
     February):39.
          Brief mention of <u>Flight to Canada</u>: "This is the fifth
     novel by one of this generation's most imaginative writers.
     The novel's background is the Civil War and Emancipation
     period, but it is also before and since and now."

3   ANON. "Ishmael Reed." <u>Yale Alumni Magazine and Journal</u>
     (March):no pagination.
          Notes Reed read his works and was sponsored by the Afro-
     American Studies and Afro-American Cultural Center.

4   ANON. "The KPFA Poetry Festival." <u>KPFA Folio</u> (May):6-7.
          Discussion of the poets who participated in the Festival.
     Reed is described as "one of the West Coast's most distin-
     guished writers. . . . In his poetry, Reed displays his
     mastery of 'HooDoo surrealism' and the Black American
     idiom." <u>Yardbird Reader</u> is "one of America's most signifi-
     cant literary periodicals and the nation's major truly
     multi-cultural anthology."

5   ANON. "Paperbacks: New and Noteworthy." <u>New York Times Book
     Review</u>, 13 November, p. 89.
          Lists <u>Flight to Canada</u>, saying that it is "comic,
     anachronistic, a spoof."

6   ANON. "P.E.N. Postscript." <u>Houston Post</u>, 27 November, p. 11.
          Reporting on the Southwest Regional P.E.N. Conference,
     makes reference to Reed's (by name only) participation in
     the conference.

7   ANON. "Reed, Ishmael 1938- ." In <u>Contemporary Authors: A
     Bio-Bibliographical Guide to Current Authors and Their
     Works</u>. Edited by Christine Nasso. Vols. 21-24. Detroit,
     Mich.: Gale Research Co., pp. 714-15.
     Biographical and bibliographical listing.

8   ANON. "Reed, Ishmael." In <u>Who's Who in America</u>. New York:
     Marquis, p. 2591.
     Biographical information listing.

9   ANON. "Reed, Ishmael. <u>Flight to Canada</u>." <u>Choice</u> 13
     (January):1439.
          Contends that <u>Flight to Canada</u> "deals more conspicuously
     [than its predecessors] with major themes, such as the pos-
     sibility of human freedom, and does it by means of novel-
     istic gambit familiar from <u>Ragtime</u>, by folding the

contemporary U.S. upon itself." Concludes by saying that "Ishmael Reed is perhaps the best of the current black poets--whatever that may mean--and no mean novelist as well."

10 ANON. "Reed, Ishmael. Shrovetide in Old New Orleans."
   Kirkus Review 45 (1 December):1312.
       Brief notice. States that Reed's efforts are contained within the "equation that everything white or Western is sterile, played out, and everything to do with folklore is the true path toward spiritual purity." The reviewer finds that Reed has an impeccable ear for contemporary slang and phrasing, but "it does not mask the emptiness of some of his attacks." He concludes: "But self-congratulation rules, and the judgments Reed means to be controversial and provocative are merely ill-considered."

11 ANON. "Uptown, Downtown: Good and Dirty." (Berkeley) Daily
   Californian, 15 April, p. 24.
       Reports on Reed's latest set-to with the English depart-ment at the University of California at Berkeley. A group of his writing students put together an anthology of their creative output but were turned down for funding to publish. English department chair Ralph Rader is quoted as say-ing "There wouldn't be much interest in it. It's hard enough to get students to read Faulkner and the classics."

12 ANON. "Writer's Writers." New York Times Book Review,
   4 December, pp. 3+.
       Many authors describe other authors whom they admire or who have influenced their work. Reed indicates his admira-tion for John A. Williams. "He's kind of like Archie Moore, whom a couple of generations of world champions ducked because not only was he a professional, with a poetic style, who could talk real pretty, but he could get up from the canvas and knock you out."

13 ARMSTRONG, DAVID. "Ishmael Reed's Yardbird Press."
   Bookswest 1, no. 6 (September/October):7, 17.
       Discusses the impact of Reed's various publishing ven-tures including Yardbird Reader, and his publishing com-pany Reed, Cannon and Johnson, and announces the forthcom-ing Calafia, an anthology of poetry, as well as Y'Bird and The Steve Cannon Show. This article, with many quotations from Reed concerning the cultural bias of the Eastern es-tablishment publishing houses, points out that Yardbird Reader won two Pushcart awards for small press writing and

1977

that the various Reed enterprises have received liberal grants from the National Endowment for the Humanities and the California Arts Council.

14   BARBER, PEGGY. "Few Giggles from Three Humorists." Cincinnati Post, 22 January, no pagination.
      Comparing Brautigan's Sombrero Fallout, A Japanese Novel, Vonnegut's Slapstick, or Lonesome No More, and Reed's Flight to Canada, Barber finds the events of the 70s have sapped "our humor . . . and the latest novels from America's leading humorists stimulate few giggles, much less laughs. Even the satire sags."

15   BATCHELOR, JOHN CALVIN. "Books: Flight to Canada." Head 2 (January/February):29, 74.
      Batchelor praises Reed's style and technique in Flight to Canada and takes the Doctorow-hypers to task. He finds Ragtime a poor substitute for the Reed original in both Flight and in Mumbo Jumbo. Batchelor dubs Reed's story-telling technique "mock 'n mold history."

16   BRESNICK, PAUL. "Ishmael Reed's Flight to Canada." New York Arts Journal 2 (Spring):32-33.
      A far-reaching evaluation of Reed as novelist in the context of a review of Flight to Canada. "Reed isn't at all concerned with the traditional premise of fiction, the registration of the individual consciousness. He opens fictional art to the forms and mythic possibilities of popular culture, pursuing not psychological description, but a perspective on history. He belongs in the company of Burroughs and Pynchon." In concluding, Bresnick asserts that "plugged into powerful energy sources, he [Reed] is perhaps the only American writer who is keeping our fiction alive."

17   CANNON, STEVE. "The Search for Baaad America." Boston Phoenix, 5 April, pp. 18, 20.
      Reviews Flight to Canada and reports an interview with Reed.

18   CHAMBERLAIN, E. L. "Reed, Ishmael. Flight to Canada." Best Sellers 36 (January):320.
      Chamberlain doesn't quite know how to deal with the novel: "Reed is an accomplished poet and there is always a message behind his stories, yet his prose can be most confusing. . . . An allegory needs a hero . . . who is the hero?"

1977

19   DESRUISSEAUX, PAUL. "Telling Tales Out of School." <u>California</u>
     <u>Monthly</u> (January-February):7.
          Highlights the inclusion of Berkeley student writers in
     <u>Yardbird Reader</u>, volume five. Reed states "when I find
     good writing, I want to get it published. I don't care
     who it's by. I think the writer ought to be read and
     encouraged.

20   DOVE, RITA, and VIEBAHN, FRED. "Geschichte ist unser Herz-
     schlag" [History is Our Heartbeat]. <u>Akzente</u> 24, no. 6:
     514-35.
          A far-ranging review of black literature in America that
     discusses the many major contributors to black letters.
     Reed is included as a substantial figure in the development
     of the literature. (Article in German.)

21   EWING, JON. "The Great Tenure Battle of 1977." <u>Daily Cali-</u>
     <u>fornian Friday Magazine: A Journal of Art and Politics</u> 3,
     no. 4 (28 January):1, 11, 13, 15.
          This interview was conducted immediately after Reed was
     denied tenure at the University of California at Berkeley.
     It touches on many aspects of a contemporary avant-garde
     writer caught in traditional departments of literature at
     major American universities. The interview also touches on
     matters of culture and several of Reed's novels, including
     <u>Flight to Canada</u>, which had been published just prior to
     the interview, <u>Free-Lance Pallbearers</u> and Reed's efforts
     to make a screenplay of it, <u>Mumbo Jumbo</u>, and <u>Yellow Back</u>
     <u>Radio</u>. Of his attempts to write a screenplay, Reed says
     "It took me time to adjust to another medium, visual. I
     like to do dazzling things for the reader. I'm a book man,
     not a film man."

22   _____. "The Great Tenure Battle of 1977." Reprinted in
     <u>Shrovetide in Old New Orleans</u>, I.25.

23   No entry.

24   FABRE, MICHEL. "Ishmael Reed's <u>Free-Lance Pallbearers</u>: On
     the Dialectics of Shit." <u>Obsidian</u> 3, no. iii:5-19.
          English translation of 1976.19.

*25 FOX, ROBERT ELLIOT. "The Logic of the White Castle: Western
     Critical Standards and the Dilemma of Black Art." <u>Obsidian</u>
     3, no. ii:18-27.
          Cited in 1978.38.

1977

26 FRASER, C. GERALD. "Black Poets Read Their Work in Cultural
       Festival at Columbia." New York Times, 28 October, p. C23.
          Reports on a poetry program to take place at Columbia.
       "Mr. Reed, who is now 39 years old, has been described by
       some critics as perhaps the best black poet writing today."

27 HOUSTON, HELEN RUTH. "Ishmael Reed." In The Afro-American
       Novel 1965-1975: A Descriptive Bibliography of Primary and
       Secondary Material. Troy, N.Y.: Whitson Publishing Co.,
       pp. 140-49.
          Brief annotations of a selected list of Reed's works and
       articles about them.

28 JONES, EARL A. "The Gloom of Being Black and in English."
       (Berkeley) Daily Californian, 4 February, p. 5.
          An editorial commentary on the effect of Reed's tenure
       denial by the English department faculty at UC Berkeley on
       one of the three black students within the department.

29 KLINKOWITZ, JEROME. The Life of Fiction. Urbana: University
       of Illinois Press, pp. 117-27.
          Reveals Reed's fiction and philosophy through short ex-
       cerpts from several of his writings. In his brief comments
       which head the chapter on Reed, Klinkowitz states that
       "Although as a black author he feels particularly em-
       battled, [Reed] sees original black writing as one element
       among many in indigenous American art." Klinkowitz also
       describes the NeoHooDoo Aesthetic as being "Reed's term for
       his own fictional plan. It expresses his allegiance both
       to an indigenous art form and to the supra-representational
       goals of that art."

30 KLOTMAN, PHYLLIS RAUCH. Another Man Gone: The Black Runner
       in Contemporary Afro-American Literature. Port Washington,
       N.Y.: Kennikat Press, p. 7.
          Brief mention in the introduction. Reed's Loop Garoo
       "deserves a thorough examination as a unique runner who
       does not fit neatly into any category." Yellow Back Radio
       Broke-Down is a novel that "reverses the most valued sym-
       bols of Western Literature and satirizes every institution
       known to white society."

31 KOHL, HERB. "Poets and Poetry." Teacher 94 (April):48-50,
       55-56.
          Quotes Reed concerning his feelings on the relationship
       between thought and feeling and what is written: "Poetry
       comes from the heart--it's like magic and it depends on
       sincerity and on inspiration."

32   LARSON, CHARLES R. "<u>Mumbo Jumbo</u>." In <u>Survey of Contemporary</u>
      <u>Literature</u>. Rev. ed. Edited by Frank N. Magill. Engle-
      wood Cliffs, N.J.: Salem Press, pp. 5139-41.
         Offers a lengthy synopsis of <u>Mumbo Jumbo</u> and a brief
      comment on the novel. Larson criticizes Reed's use of
      photographs in the novel: "Numerous photographs and
      quotations from other books punctuate the text of <u>Mumbo</u>
      <u>Jumbo</u>, often marring the narrative by contributing little
      more than general obscurity."

33   McBRIDE, EARNEST L. "Black Writer Raps to 300 at U.S.C."
      <u>Los Angeles Sentinel</u>, 19 May, Section A, p. 9.
         Writes of hearing Reed at a lecture/reading at USC. The
      audience is described as "mostly white" and "slow to re-
      spond." Reed "entertained . . . with bullet-like barks of
      understatement and spurious comparisons between the Bay
      Area and Southern California." McBride contends that Reed
      cares only about money. "Like so many other 'pragmatic'
      black celebrities, Reed today is being guided by one great
      symbol--the dollar sign." McBride claims Reed gives short
      shrift to the intellectual development of black people
      within the United States: "If we had a dollar for every
      Black intellectual, we could set up a world bank."

34   NAZARETH, PETER. "The Phenomenon of <u>Roots</u>. <u>Afriscope</u> 7
      (May):37, 39-40, 42.
         Nazareth compares and reviews <u>Roots</u> and <u>Flight to Canada</u>.
      He points out that the phenomenon of <u>Roots</u> has a tradition
      that has been overlooked and even a contemporary counter-
      part, Reed's <u>Flight to Canada</u>. Nazareth quotes extensively
      from Reed's speech to the Third World Writers Conference.

35   NORTHOUSE, CAMERON. "Ishmael Reed." In <u>Conversations with</u>
      <u>Writers II</u>. Detroit, Mich.: Gale Research Co., pp. 212-54.
         The interview explores in depth Reed's views on writing
      in America, literary criticism, and publishing problems of
      young, contemporary, avant-garde artists. Reed says of
      art, in general, that "we think there's a new art that is
      everything, when it is going to be mixed up. It's going to
      get into writing, and music--well, music has always been
      that way." On the traditional novel Reed comments, "I
      think by the time a novel is finished, I find it boring
      now. . . . But novels are going to have to do much more.
      As a matter of fact, I don't even think we're going to call
      them novels anymore. . . . I find myself restless and
      anxious about the novel as it has been done: just page
      after page of this dry type--predictable--I mean, formula,
      the scenery, the characterization, and everything." The

1977

interview relates an anecdote about the jacket notes to
Chattanooga and opens with comment about those notes.

36 PAGE, JAMES ALLEN. Selected Black American Writers. Boston,
    Mass.: G. K. Hall, p. 229.
        Brief biographical facts, highly selective bibliographic
    listing of primary works.

37 ROCHMIS, DOROTHY H. "Flight to Canada by Ishmael Reed." West
    Coast Review of Books 3, no. 1:24.
        In a short notice, Rochmis asserts that this is "a novel
    injected with enormous humor. . . . Reed has taken all
    kinds of liberties with his fanciful approach to the pe-
    riod and the result is this quite unusual and delightful
    novel."

38 SHAGASS, KATHY. "Ishmael Reed Charges, 'Naropa is a con
    job.'" Berkeley Barb, 25 November–1 December, p. 11.
        Reports Reed's opinions regarding the Naropa Institute
    in Boulder, Colorado. The article makes reference to
    Reed's "passion for exposing phony spiritualism," and
    quotes him extensively about literature, Afro-American
    writers, and the already-pervasive Hoodoo force.

39 STEWART, J. T. "Satiric, Surrealistic Attack on Old Values."
    Seattle Times, 23 January, no pagination.
        Praises Flight to Canada as the fifth novel of Reed's
    canon. Stewart finds the novel concerned with "apathy and
    complacency in contemporary society." The reviewer asserts
    that Reed is a prolific and influential black writer, con-
    cluding that "Anyone who reads [Reed's] hip non-traditional
    style can expect an attack on conventional values and tra-
    ditional assumptions."

40 TURNER, DARWIN T. "Black Fiction: History and Myth."
    Studies in American Fiction 5, no. 1:109–26.
        In this lengthy review of black novels of significance
    for the past century, Turner finds Reed's works to be in a
    continuum of black literary history: the historical novel,
    and the myth-making novel. Turner discusses both Mumbo
    Jumbo and Last Days of Louisiana Red.

41 UPHAUS, SUZANNE HENNING. "Ishmael Reed's Canada." Canadian
    Review of American Studies 8 (Spring):95–99.
        Uphaus uses the metaphor of Canada as freedom land found
    in Reed's Flight to Canada to offer an interesting plot
    summary, but leaves one somewhat disappointed as her ap-
    proach does not really deal with a Canadian's view of

Reed's novel of the broader issue: Canada as land of
refuge for Americans on the run. Perhaps her reinforcement
of Canada as a land as racist as America does offer sure
myth-busting, but Reed and others have already done that.

42 WEISS, MICHAEL. "The Politics of Pedantry." New West 2
(17 January):NC-5-8.
A news feature comparing Reed's tenure denial with the
tenure denial of Harry Edwards at UC Berkeley. The feature
attempts some in-depth investigative reporting.

43 WOOD, CRAIG. "A Man for All Seasons." Reno Evening Gazette,
25 April, p. 13.
Wood spotlights Reed's reading of poetry at the University of Nevada. He finds Reed's poetry to be simple,
rhetorically. In sum, Reed offers "the calm words of a
gentle man." Reed incorporates and anticipates; "Reed, as
an urban poet and a voice of the emerging generation, reflects more than anything, growth and progress."

1978

1 ANGELOU, MAYA. "West Coast Literary Lions." Saturday Review
5 (11 November):60.
Sees Yardbird Lives! as a successful example of an
anthology: "A rich and well-paced anthology offers the
best in private sensuality. A reader can indulge in one
author's bitter threnodial prose then in minutes turn a
page to the high clear sound of lyrical poetry. A good
anthology also introduces little-known but worthy new
writers. Yardbird Lives! succeeds in both areas."

2 _____. "Yardbird Lives!" City Miner 3:1.
Reprints Angelou's review of Yardbird Lives! (1978.1).

3 ANON. "Ishmael Reed." Two Hands News and Chicago Poetry
Calendar (June):1-3.
Reports Reed's reading at the University of Illinois on
April 17, 1978. It includes excerpts of the works he read.
The reviewer recommends Y'Bird and most particularly the
Reed/Ellison interview which appears there.

4 ANON. "Paperbacks: New and Noteworthy." New York Times Book
Review, 26 March, p. 29.
Short notice of the paperback publication of Mumbo Jumbo:
"Ishmael Reed created a free-wheeling myth of his own, com-
pounded of highbrow satire, low-key farce--even roman à
clef."

1978

5   ANON. "Reed, Ishmael. <u>Shrovetide in Old New Orleans</u>."
     <u>Booklist</u> 74 (15 February):971.
          Asserts that "the scope and vitality of the selections
     should intrigue Reed's following and be arresting to the
     uninitiated."

6   ANON. "Reed, Ishmael. <u>Shrovetide in Old New Orleans</u>."
     <u>Choice</u> 15, no. 7 (September):874.
          Views Reed as "able to make readers interested in his
     perceptions of life . . . a perceptive critic of Afro-
     American authors."

7   ANON. "<u>Shrovetide in Old New Orleans</u> by Ishmael Reed."
     <u>Virginia Quarterly Review</u> (Summer):no pagination.
          Brief comment. The essays "form a recent autobiographi-
     cal portrait of a penetrating mind thoroughly engaged in
     intimate, provocative, and humorous acts of vision."

8   ARATA, ESTHER SPRING. <u>More Black American Playwrights: A
     Bibliography</u>. Metuchen, N.J.: Scarecrow Press,
     pp. 167-68.
          Makes reference to filmscript of <u>Yellow Back Radio
     Broke-Down</u>.

9   BADGER, DAVID. "<u>Shrovetide in Old New Orleans</u>." <u>Nashville
     Tennessean</u>, 2 April, no pagination.
          Finds the volume to be "a stockpile . . . dry-as-dust."

10   BELKIND, ALLEN. "Ishmael Reed. <u>Shrovetide in Old New
     Orleans</u>." <u>World Literature Today</u> 52 (Autumn):635.
          Asserts that Reed has "emerged as one of the more
     promising and prolific of the current young black writers
     in America." Belkind gives a brief overview of the book's
     contents, and concludes that "Reed's collection offers
     many useful insights into current Afro-American culture.
     It is also a useful purgative for white complacency and
     an interesting self-portrait of a complex and talented
     black writer struggling for understanding and success on
     his own terms."

11   BOEPPLE, BOB. "Voice of '60s Returns." <u>Shreveport Journal</u>,
     24 March, no pagination.
          Describes <u>Shrovetide in Old New Orleans</u> as "an interest-
     ing collection. . . . Many of the 32 essays are really
     fun."

1978

12   BRUNSDALE, MITZI. "Reed's 'Spiritual Autobiography' Stirs
         Things Up." Houston Post, 7 May, no pagination.
             Views Shrovetide in Old New Orleans as both brilliant
         and dangerous. She praises Reed for his style and par-
         ticularly points to the title essay, "Shrovetide in Old
         New Orleans" as an example of his fine style and his
         ability to give a hot and cool account of New Orleans.
         Brunsdale takes Reed to task for suggesting a hunt to
         "expose the cultural Nazis" which emulates "the hysterical
         paranoia of the Nazi himself."

13   CALLAHAN, ROBERT et al. "Interview." In Before Columbus
         Foundation Catalog One: Contemporary American Literature
         1978-1979. Berkeley, Calif.: Before Columbus Foundation,
         pp. 1-12.
             Far-ranging interview which besides Callahan and Reed
         includes Simon Ortiz, Shawn Hsu Wong, David Meltzer, and
         Victor Hernandez Cruz. Reed discusses the start of the
         Before Columbus Foundation, his concept of Hoodoo. Many
         subjects are brought up and discussed.

14   DAVIS, ARTHUR P. "Novels of the New Black Renaissance (1960-
         1977): A Thematic Survey." CLA Journal 21, no. 4 (June):
         457-90.
             Davis's lengthy article reviews and shows examples from
         writers who are, according to this author, part of the New
         Black Renaissance, a movement more vigorous than its prede-
         cessor, the New Negro Movement of the 1920s. The article
         includes most of those authors who have contributed to the
         movement, including Ishmael Reed. Reed's section discusses
         Yellow Back Radio Broke-Down, "Neo Hoodoo Manifesto," and
         Flight to Canada. In reference to Yellow Back Radio, Davis
         says "I am not sure I understand it, and this goes for most
         of the author's works." Later he states "No other writer
         of the past era has written anything quite like it." Davis
         does not particularly like Louisiana Red because it has
         very little depth. "It may be that the comic-book-style
         plot is required for his purpose, but it still strikes the
         reader--at least some readers--as being overdone. Nothing
         that Ishmael Reed writes is ever dull, but cleverness is
         not enough." In his discussion of Flight to Canada, Davis
         finds difficulty with Reed's use of well-known historical
         personas.

1978

15 DOMINI, JOHN. "Ishmael Reed: A Conversation with John
        Domini." American Poetry Review 7:32-36.
            Domini and Reed have a far-ranging discussion which
        includes, among others, talk of the differences between big
        press and small press publishing, Berkeley counterculture,
        Yardbird Wing Editions, Reed's reception by the critics,
        and mention of many of Reed's works. The interview offers
        further insight into the motivations and development of the
        author.

16 DUFF, GERALD. "Ishmael Reed." In American Novelists Since
        World War II. Edited by Jeffrey Helterman and Richard
        Layman. Detroit, Mich.: Bruccoli Clark/Gale Research Co.,
        pp. 417-22.
            Brief survey of each of the five Reed novels and a scant
        exploration of critical opinion of each novel. Includes
        brief bibliography of works discussed and a few critical
        articles.

17 FAIRBANKS, CAROL, and ENGELDINGER, EUGENE A. Black American
        Fiction: A Bibliography. Metuchen, N.J.: Scarecrow
        Press, pp. 240-43.
            Selected listing of Reed's works and critical comment on
        them.

18 FARNSWORTH, ROBERT M. "Shrovetide in Old New Orleans by
        Ishmael Reed." New Letters 45:120-21.
            Farnsworth calls Reed "a businessman, a poet, an irasci-
        ble polemicist, and a staunch friend" and describes Shrove-
        tide in Old New Orleans as a "Vodoun mixture of scholar-
        ship, wit, personal statements and at its best--prophecy."

19 FELD, DAVID. "Ethnic Mumbo Jumbo." (Berkeley) Daily
        Californian, 21 April, pp. 25-26.
            Proposes that all of the pieces in Shrovetide in Old New
        Orleans are reworkings of the same basic theme: "There is
        a great artistic tradition among non-white people in this
        country that is constantly under attack by 'the white lit-
        erary mob.'" The author states at the beginning that
        "Ishmael Reed is one of the country's best and most influ-
        ential writers" but concludes that "I look forward to
        Reed's next novel, but I don't think I'll read his essays
        again."

1978

20 FONTENOT, CHESTER J. "Ishmael Reed and the Politics of
    Aesthetics, or Shake Hands and Come Out Conjuring."
    <u>Black American Literature Forum</u> 12:20-23.
        Fontenot attempts to bridge the world vision of Reed
    and the academics' delight in trying to place all black
    writers into the mode of social critics. Fontenot finds
    Reed a social critic, one whose criticism ignores the tra-
    ditional modes of social criticism by bringing to black
    literature the aesthetic of diasporic African culture and
    neo-hoodooism. The article concentrates on Reed's poetry
    for the bulk of examples.

21 GATES, HENRY-LOUIS. "<u>Flight to Canada</u> by Ishmael Reed."
    <u>Journal of Negro History</u> 63 (January):78-81.
        Gates comments on the novel, bringing an intelligent
    sense of history to the works of Reed and Reed's place in
    American letters. Of the novel, he observes that it is "a
    major work . . . one senses here a sort of ending: . . .
    for the search for the word, which Reed began in <u>Mumbo
    Jumbo</u>, has realized itself finally in the successful search
    for the text. . . ."

22 _____. "Parody of Forms." <u>Saturday Review</u> 5 (4 March):28.
        Uses the opportunity of reviewing <u>Shrovetide in Old New
    Orleans</u> to make some salient observations about Reed's
    writing in general. Gates notes that Reed is far from a
    satirist in the derogatory sense; he uses the subtle satir-
    ical parody, a satire of forms. Reed has "altered our
    notions of what is possible in black fiction," more than
    Morrison, Gaines, Jones, or Walker. He finds <u>Shrovetide</u> a
    motley collection of essays unified by Reed's essay on
    Vodoun, and his reviews of the work of Chester Himes and
    Wright's <u>Native Son</u>. The total collection offers a demon-
    stration of how Reed's use of Vodoun has "become his meta-
    phor for the black man and essential philosophical frame-
    work for his fiction." It should be noted that substantial
    sections of Gates's review of <u>Flight to Canada</u> (see
    1978.15) have been included here.

23 GOODMAN, MICHAEL. "Conjuring With Words." <u>Newsday</u>, 19 March,
    no pagination.
        <u>Shrovetide in Old New Orleans</u> is found to be "unpre-
    dictable, lively and thought-provoking"; "one is impressed
    by Reed's humanity, courage, individualism."

117

1978

24 GOVER, ROBERT. "An Interview With Ishmael Reed." <u>Black</u>
    <u>American Literature Forum</u> 12:12-19.
        Gover opens his article with a zinger from Reed ("I'm
    not against Christianity, I only want to <u>humble</u> it, like
    it says it ought to be") and follows with a discourse on
    how he managed to get this article together, interspersed
    with Reed's comments. Gover notes in this beginning that
    "What puzzles me is that the bookselling machine has not
    yet exploited the natural, built-in box office potential
    of Ishmael Reed. The star-making system was practically
    invented to sell books and records and movies, and here
    they have this lively contender for the crown, and what
    are they doing?" Reed talks about <u>Mumbo Jumbo</u> and <u>Last</u>
    <u>Days of Louisiana Red</u>, saying "<u>Louisiana Red</u> is a casual
    use of the Voodoo esthetic, whereas <u>Mumbo Jumbo</u> was more
    formalized." Voodoo, writing, and Norman Mailer are dis-
    cussed at length. As with all the interviews with Reed,
    many things are touched upon.

25 GRIFFIN, L. W. "Reed, Ishmael. <u>Shrovetide in Old New</u>
    <u>Orleans</u>." <u>Library Journal</u> 103 (1 February):366.
        Briefly describes the collection. Concludes that this
    is a "lively, opinionated view of black and other minority
    writers in America."

26 GUERESCHI, EDWARD. "Reed, Ishmael. <u>Shrovetide in Old New</u>
    <u>Orleans</u>." <u>Best Sellers</u> 38 (May):52.
        Talks of Reed as representing "the new generation of
    black writers who have moved beyond the confrontation
    politics of the Sixties" and as maintaining "an exuberant
    independence from all factions." Guereschi praises <u>Shrove-</u>
    <u>tide</u> as being "an impressive a feat as James Baldwin's <u>The</u>
    <u>Fire Next Time</u> (1962)." He concludes that "Reed may draw
    controversy to himself deliberately, yet his sense of
    style, intellectual wit, and playfulness create the climate
    for fresh evaluation."

27 HARRIS, JESSICA. "<u>Shrovetide in Old New Orleans</u> by Ishmael
    Reed." <u>Essence</u> 8 (April):41.
        Commends Reed as "perhaps the most original of contempo-
    rary American writers" and characterizes <u>Shrovetide</u> as
    being a "guided tour through Reed's mind." Harris con-
    cludes: "You may agree or disagree with Reed, but you
    won't be indifferent because he's sure to touch your mind."

1978

28   HARRIS, PHILIP. "Call Him Ishmael." (Cambridge, Mass.) <u>Real
     Paper</u>, 25 February, pp. 25+.
         On the occasion of the publication of <u>Shrovetide in Old
     New Orleans</u>, Harris interviewed Reed in Berkeley. Reed is
     described as "the brilliant writer whose linguistic pyro-
     technics and blazing satire . . . captured the imagination
     of so many readers." Reed's remarks range over his
     career, his view of the publishing, literary and educa-
     tional establishments, and his own work.

29   HELM, MICHAEL. "Ishmael Reed: An Interview." <u>City Miner</u> 3,
     no. 4:1-9, 37-42.
         Attempts to strike a balance between all of the artistic,
     political, and aesthetic aspects of Reed. Reed conveys his
     ideas on the current state of the arts and their future
     role in American society. Reed also levels his sights on
     the current political situation, noting that the United
     States needs "some kind of socialistic base . . . so that
     people are guaranteed an adequate standard of existence."

30   HICKS, JACK. "A One-Man Heathen Horde." <u>Nation</u> 266, no. 9
     (11 March):277.
         Finds <u>Shrovetide</u> to contain examples of Reed at his
     best. Hicks notes that Reed often spreads himself too
     thin as evidenced by some of the book reviews included in
     the collection. He further points out that Reed hasn't
     the patience of the fine essayists because his essays often
     lack the conventional connective tissue the form requires.
     On the whole, Hicks finds Reed's prose "a pleasure to read,
     filled with little veins of energy and irritation."

31   HOGAN, WILLIAM. "Files on Parade." <u>San Francisco Chronicle</u>,
     3 February, p. 49.
         In a review of <u>Shrovetide in Old New Orleans</u>, Hogan
     first discusses Reed, calling him "something of a literary
     eccentric," an author who "has yet to reach the literary
     status of major Black American writers." <u>Shrovetide</u> is of
     uneven quality, Hogan asserts, but the essays do "represent
     Reed's view of life, which is generally affirmative in the
     William Saroyan tradition." The review concludes: "There
     are both warmth and indignation in Ishmael Reed's lively
     prose, and a beat, like far-off jungle drums."

32   JONES, ROBERT W. "Language and Structure in Ishmael Reed's
     <u>Yellow Back Radio Broke-Down</u>." <u>Notes on Contemporary Lit-
     erature</u> 8, no. 2 (March):2-3.
         Offers several insights to <u>Yellow Back Radio</u> and its
     unification of theme through structure and language. He

1978

contends that Reed's language is similar to a Coltrane
concerto or a Lou Rawls monologue. Jones writes that because Reed is a poet first, "he is able to couple disci-
pline and chaos and come out with a unified whole." He
sums up his notes by adding that "language unites Reed's
attempt to write a protest novel without having it fall
into stark polemic . . . a novel whose superficial ap-
pearance of chaotic motion and mumbling Hoo-Dooism ulti-
mately achieve a unified form worthy of critical attention."

33 KAISER, ERNEST. "Recent Books: Shrovetide in Old New
Orleans." Freedomways 18, no. 3 (Third Quarter):181–82.
Argues that in Shrovetide in Old New Orleans Reed's
"right wing, anti-Communist views . . . have come to full
bloom." Concludes that "Reed's know-nothing, right-wing,
anti-black cynicism is paying off."

34 KATZ, WILLIAM, and RICHARDS, BERRY G. Magazines for Libraries.
New York: R. R. Bowker Co., p. 583.
Short notice on Y'Bird. "This is the traditional revolutionary cry of Americans to be Americans and enjoy their
own art instead of depending upon what Reed calls 'Euro-
philes'. . . . This is a superior review/little magazine,
which should get wide support."

35 KEIYA. "A Review of Ishmael Reed's Flight to Canada."
Obsidian 4:118–19.
Provides an enthusiastic view of Flight to Canada.
Keiya notes that this work, published during the bicen-
tennial, explicates the last two hundred years of American
hisotry. It is, according to him, "a can't put down, don't
want to put down, book."

36 KENT, GEORGE E. "Freewheeling Excursions Into Black Art,
Politics." Chicago Tribune, 26 February, Section 7, p. 3.
Thoroughly examines Shrovetide in Old New Orleans, look-
ing at both individual pieces and the work as a whole: "I
found . . . that by cross-referencing stances taken in
several essays additional contexts could be found." Kent
scores the omission of any serious dealing with economic
matters. "Nonetheless, as Reed suggested in his introduction, he stirs things up a bit."

37 LARSON, CHARLES. "Ishmael Reed's Defiant Voice." Washington
Post, 2 April, Section E, p. 7.
Gives a lengthy discussion of Shrovetide in Old New
Orleans, finding it to contain the same fresh, prolific,
outspoken Reed that readers have come to expect. However,

Larson compares Reed, the man of letters, to Leslie
Fiedler, describing them both as "the good/bad boys of
American Letters." He takes Reed to task for reprinting
the interview with Jon Ewing (1977.12) when Reed's tenure
was denied by UC Berkeley. Larson concludes his review
by saying that Shrovetide "is meant to be savored slowly,
dipped into from time to time. No matter whether we agree
with him or not, Ishmael Reed is always entertaining, often
provocative, at times profound."

38 McCABE, CAROL. "By Ishmael Reed, Black Surrealist."
Providence (R.I.) Journal, 18 June, no pagination.
    Praises Reed as a poet and novelist. McCabe finds
Shrovetide in Old New Orleans to be pompous, the antithesis
of Reed's tone in his novels. She does grant that Reed
needed to have the chance to do a book like Shrovetide, but
urges Reed to return to his forte: "That fictional space
to which only he can take us to hear the birds and see the
lights."

39 MACKEY, NATHANIEL. "Ishmael Reed and the Black Aesthetic."
CLA Journal 21, no. 3 (March):355-66.
    Provides an apology for the aesthetic Hoo-Dooism, the
Reed credo. Mackey differentiates between the Reed panoply
of aesthetics and the more monolithic approach of the Black
Aesthetics advocates such as Larry Neal, Addison Gayle, and
Hoyt Fuller. He finds ways to clearly define the numerous
differences including a view of "art for art's sake" em-
braced by Reed and generally opposed by Black Aesthetics,
and the need for social consciousness writing which Reed
has clearly criticized on numerous occasions. Mackey's
breadth of knowledge of Reed's work is clearly evident as
is his understanding of the principal feuds within the
current wave of black artists. His work adds understanding
and clarity to a difficult subject.

40 MAZORAL, LOUISE. "Shrovetide in Old New Orleans."
Charleston (S.C.) News and Courier, 30 April, no pagination.
    Very brief notice. The book is characterized as "writ-
ten in an explosive style that completely disregards rules
of grammar. The result is incoherent and difficult to
read."

41 NADLE, MARLENE. "Ishmael Reed Conjures Up A Voodoo Cure for
    Black America." <u>Politicks and Other Human Interests</u> 1
    (25 April):22-23.
        In an essay-interview, Nadle attempts to integrate the
    literary Reed with the ideological Reed. As a result of her
    interview and readings of Reed, she concludes: "Reed was
    finally no more optimistic than I . . . . I remembered that,
    in Reed's books, hoodooism never triumphs. His artistic
    honesty demanded that the forces of the dominant culture
    defeat it in the end." Nadle admits to seeking answers
    from Reed. She questioned him closely on his opinions and
    outlook for the economic and intellectual growth and devel-
    opment of black culture in the 1970s. She also concludes
    that Reed's "verbal voodist cure for America reads: once
    you change the consciousness, you change the politics.

42 NAZARETH, PETER. "Time in the Third World: A Fictional Ex-
    ploration." In <u>The Awakened Conscience</u>. Edited by C. D.
    Narasimhaiah. New Delhi, India: Sterling, pp. 195-205.
        Incorporates the notion of time in Reed's novel as an
    example of a Third World writer living in the First World
    but who relies on the sensibility of a Third World people
    (African) from which to draw his aesthetics. Nazareth
    draws his examples from <u>The Last Days of Louisiana Red</u> and
    <u>Yellow Back Radio Broke-Down</u>.

43 NELHAUS, ARLYNN. "<u>Shrovetide</u> Infuriating, But Concise Tale."
    <u>Denver Post</u>, 23 April, no pagination.
        Nelhaus gives a rapid-fire review of <u>Shrovetide in Old
    New Orleans</u>. She finds the collection alternatingly "in-
    furiating, beautifully concise, fresh-voiced, dumb, and
    unforgettable." Her criticism stems from a desire to have
    Reed's writing in general be "not confusing gramatically
    . . . more generous in identifying the lesser known people
    [referred] to. . . . " She wishes "that Doubleday's
    editors wouldn't have allowed names to get misspelled."

44 NICHOLS, CHARLES. "Comic Modes in Black America." In <u>Comic
    Relief: Humor in Contemporary Literature</u>. Edited by Sarah
    Blacher Cohen. Urbana: University of Illinois Press,
    pp. 105-26.
        Nichols directs his comments about the comic structure
    of Reed's work to his novels, pointing out that the novel
    is Reed's métier. The comedy of Reed is farce, satire,
    conventional modes used for comic effects.

1978

45 NOLAND, THOMAS. "Reed's Volume Credo in Experimental Work."
    Anniston (Ala.) Star, 26 February, no pagination.
        Discusses Shrovetide in Old New Orleans. "While one may
    quarrel with Ishmael Reed's point of view one can't fault
    his eyesight."

46 NORDELL, RODERICK. "A Writer on the Installment Plan."
    Christian Science Monitor, 22 March, p. 31.
        Shrovetide in Old New Orleans is discussed in this short
    review. Nordell calls Reed's nonfiction a "challenge to
    stereotyped thinking," and praises Reed's "willingness to
    take unpopular stances [that] is part of his individuality."

47 OLDERMAN, RAYMOND M. "American Fiction 1974-1976: The People
    Who Fell to Earth." Contemporary Literature 19, no. 4
    (Autumn):497-527.
        Olderman's overview of fiction of the years 1974 to 1976
    is cast in the realism of the search for the movements of
    the Sixties and the manifestations of these movements' de-
    cline and withering from the contemporary scene. Olderman
    finds that the fiction of '74-'76 deals with concerns
    other than "how the world will end"; it deals with male/
    female relations, personal, sexual, racial, spiritual, and
    cosmic betrayal. Olderman includes Reed in the section on
    black writers who have moved away from the pain of the
    movement of the Sixties deflated, and have opted for build-
    ing "positive models." Reed's Flight to Canada and The
    Last Days of Louisiana Red are cited as examples of Reed's
    "comprehensive creation of a model world view which can
    reconcile his interpretation of myth and history with his
    street-wise views of the black community." In Olderman's
    comparison of concerns in Mumbo Jumbo and Louisiana Red,
    he notes that "Reed seems to be altering his perspective
    since Mumbo Jumbo, unless Louisiana Red simply reveals an
    anger with what the Berkeley scene has done to the move-
    ment." Of Flight to Canada, Olderman says it is a complex
    work, as are all Reed's works. In Flight to Canada Reed's
    "theories of history are the center focus."

48 POPKIN, MICHAEL, comp. Modern Black Writers: A Library of
    Literary Criticism. New York: Frederick Ungar Publishing
    Co., pp. 362-69.
        The portion on Reed consists solely of excerpts from
    selected articles and reviews about Reed. It offers no
    new material.

1978

49   SCHULTZ, ELIZABETH A. "The Heirs of Ralph Ellison: Patterns
       of Individualism in the Contemporary Afro-American Novel."
       CLA Journal 22:101-22.
           Reed is mentioned in a footnote (p. 105) which tells why
       the author failed to include his works in this article:
       "Ishmael Reed's Yellow Back Radio Broke-Down, Mumbo Jumbo,
       and The Last Days of Louisiana Red . . . describe a plural-
       istic society as does Ellison, but . . . do not focus on
       an individual's self-discovery."

50   SIMON, JEFF. "Ishmael Continuing His 'Neo-hoo doo.'" Buffalo
       News, 26 March, p. G-4.
           Shrovetide in Old New Orleans is "about as noisy, fierce
       and combative as such catch-alls ever get (also as funny)."
       Yet "in all of this book, there is almost no feeling of
       repose or thoughtfulness, only cerebrally incandescent
       agitation."

51   SPEARMAN, WALTER. "The Literary Lantern." (Southern Pines,
       N.C.) Pilot, 14 June, no pagination.
           Short comment on Shrovetide in Old New Orleans: the
       volume "shows [Reed] at his controversial best."

52   THOMAS, PHIL. "Reed Leads a Tour Inside Black Life." Omaha
       World-Herald, 2 April, no pagination.
           Discusses Shrovetide in Old New Orleans. Reed "writes
       in a highly personal, impressionistic style that takes a
       bit of getting used to, but once understood, the rewards
       to the reader are great."

53   _____. "Shrovetide in Old New Orleans by Ishmael Reed."
       (Monterey, Penn.) Peninsula Herald, 9 April, no pagination.
       Reprint of 1978.52.

54   WATKINS, MEL. "Reed Reader: Shrovetide in Old New Orleans."
       New York Times Book Review, 12 March, Section 7, pp. 11,
       24.
           Watkins finds Shrovetide in Old New Orleans to be typi-
       cal Reed, but also finds the collection of essays lacking
       in logic and ultimately not persuasive. "For those who
       come fresh to this material it may be as controversial and
       stirring as Reed intended. If you're familiar with it,
       however, for the most part you'll just have to content
       yourself watching Ishmael Reed floating and stinging."
       Watkins observes that this collection does not achieve the
       status of an "intellectual autobiography" which Reed at-
       tempts to achieve. "Some of the selections--particularly
       the book reviews--are simply too thin."

1979

55 WEIXLMAN, JOE; FIKES, ROBERT, Jr.; and REED, ISHMAEL. "Mapping Out the Gumbo Works: An Ishmael Reed Bibliography." Black American Literature Forum 12:24-29.
   Weixlman et al. set out to "catalogue all of the published and soon-to-be published writings by and about Ishmael Reed." The unannotated bibliography unfortunately manages to overlook such significant items as the Spanish edition of Mumbo Jumbo and the numerous reprintings of Reed's poems in anthologies.

56 WHITNEY, VALERIE. "Reed's Autobiography Drifts Into Black American History." Washington Afro-American, 12 August, no pagination.
   Whitney recommends Shrovetide in Old New Orleans to Reed's avid fans as one that should not be missed. He highlights the content of the collection noting that the time frame, 1971-1977, is "only a formality when one considers the subject as a whole."

1979

1 ANON. "Bay Area author Ishmael Reed." Oakland Public Library Association Newsletter 8 (Summer):4.
   Reports Reed's remarks at the Author's Guild of America.

2 ANON. "Calafia, The California Poetry." Small Press Review 11 (September):no pagination.
   Finds the book "a lot of good reading and a significant collection."

3 ANON. "Reed, Ishmael. A Secretary To The Spirits." Booklist (15 February):909.
   Short notice. "Master of ceremonies Reed . . . strikes up the blues rhythms . . . then black humor, and a rogue's bestiary of 'bad press' wolves, waterbuggers, envious vampires, landlord rats, corporate cats, wily crows, and avenging ravens to instruct his audience. Ishmael's 'beastly' fables contain not a little black-is-beautiful moralizing." Concludes that the volume is "serious social comedy in verse."

4 ANON. "A Selection of Recent Paperbacks: Shrovetide in Old New Orleans." Washington Star, 11 March, no pagination.
   Finds Shrovetide "delightful access to a writer whose fiction is not always the most accessible."

1979

5   BAIN, ROBERT. "Ishmael Reed." In <u>Southern Writers: A Bio-</u>
      <u>graphical Dictionary</u>. Edited by Robert Bain, Joseph Flora,
      and Louis Rubin, Jr. Baton Rouge: Louisiana State Univer-
      sity Press, pp. 377-79.
         Biographical information.

6   BEDELL, THOMAS D. "<u>Yardbird Lives!</u>" <u>Library Journal</u> 104
      (1 January):110.
         Short descriptive notice of the anthology. "Tastes will
      dictate different highs and lows, but overall this is a
      valuable collection of poems, short stories, essays,
      scenarios, and graphics."

7   CONTOSKI, VICTOR. "Reed, Ishmael, ed. and pref. <u>Calafia:</u>
      <u>The California Poetry</u>." <u>Library Journal</u> 104 (1 October):
      2103.
         <u>Calafia</u> has "much excellent, little-known poetry. . . .
      One wishes someone would mention the criteria of inclusion."

8   CROUCH, STANLEY. "The HooDoo Wrath of Ishmael Reed."
      <u>Village Voice</u> 24 (22 January):75+.
         In reviewing <u>Shrovetide in Old New Orleans</u>, Crouch points
      out flaws in some of the work's portions, notably the inter-
      views. He also attempts to explain some of Reed's notions
      of Neo-HooDooism, the relationship of black homosexual
      writers vis-à-vis a white audience, and the problems faced
      by black writers who break with convention. He notes
      "Ishmael Reed is an important contemporary voice because
      he provokes ideas and realizes that the racial situation
      in America is now as much about ideas as anything else,
      and that the black writer who breaks with convention risks
      a very special castigation." He concludes that "Reed's
      batting average is at least .450, which means he is right
      or illuminatingly suggestive four-and-one-half times out
      of ten. Human life being what it is--not to mention the
      insipidness of most racial commentary, black and white--
      seems pretty good to me."

9   ERICKSON, BARBARA. "Redefining Culture of California."
      <u>Sunday Magazine</u>, 12 August, pp. 8-9.
         Reviews <u>Calafia</u> finding it filled with contemporary
      talent as well as talent from nineteenth-century California.
      Erickson finds its format readable and filled with poems
      which still speak clearly to contemporary readers.

10   FRENCH, WILLIAM P.; FABRE, MICHEL; SINGH, AMRITJIT; and FABRE,
     GENEVIEVE E. <u>Afro-American Poetry and Drama, 1790-1975: A
     Guide to Information Sources</u>. Detroit, Mich.: Gale Re-
     search Co., pp. 25, 38, 50, 223-24, 398, 400.
          Reed's works and material about him and his work listed
     throughout.

11   FRIEDMAN, MICKEY. "The Contentious <u>State of the Language</u>."
     <u>San Francisco Examiner</u>, 12 November, p. 22.
          Reports on a symposium sponsored by the English Union
     and held in San Francisco to discuss <u>State of the Language</u>,
     a new book in which an article by Reed appears. The story
     discusses Reed's remarks at the meeting as well as the tiff
     he got into with Frederic Raphael.

12   HOGAN, WILLIAM. "Most Ambitious Anthology of Poet-Novelists."
     <u>San Francisco Chronicle</u>, 3 June, p. 58.
          Brief notice of <u>Calafia</u>. Hogan says "Is the only cul-
     tural advantage to California that you can make a right
     turn on a red light as the Woody Allen character observed
     in 'Annie Hall'? Not so, argue the poet-novelists Ishmael
     Reed and Al Young. To prove otherwise in a state where
     'the usual is the unusual,' they have come up with one of
     the most ambitious anthologies of recent years."

13   JACKSON, DAVID. "Dial 'F' for Funk." <u>Soho Weekly News</u>,
     18 October, no pagination.
          Review of the opening night of the musical group
     Parliament-Funkadelic at the Apollo. One of the band
     members' costumes was likened to "Ishmael Reed's character,
     Loop Garou, in the abstract expressionist black cowboy
     mystery novel, <u>Yellow Back Radio Broke-Down</u>."

14   JACOB, WALTER. "Reed Continues Aiding Unknowns." <u>Yale Daily
     News</u>, 28 September, p. 9.
          A news story describing Reed's discussion at Calhoun,
     Master Charles Davis's home.

15   JOHNSON, LEMUEL A. "'Aint's,' 'Us'ens,' and 'Mother Dear':
     Issues in the Language of Madhubuti, Jones, and Reed."
     <u>Journal of Black Studies</u> 10, no. 2 (December):139-66.
          This lengthy article explores the context of contempo-
     rary Afro-American literature. It examines the special
     language of Jones, Don Lee (Madhubuti), and Ishmael Reed,
     attempting to demonstrate that Jones and Madhubuti are
     forerunners of Reed's style and language. While not taking
     up the thorn-filled arguments for or against Creole, Black
     English, <u>ad infinitum</u>, it does look at the stylistic and

1979

infinitive functions of certain aspects of Afro-American
language. He says near the conclusion of the article that
"Reed's work and its language best illustrate here why a
committed person chooses the medium of literature to ex-
press his views."

16 McELROY, GARY. "Black Condition is Author's Subject."
(Miss.) Natchez Democrat, 23 March, no pagination.
McElroy reviews Shrovetide in Old New Orleans and finds
Reed an intellectual who "tends to wear his feelings, at
least about . . . race, on his shirt sleeve a bit too much
for me, but his insight, intelligent descriptive power and
savvy understanding of human nature is astounding and wel-
comed reading."

17 McKLE, KAREN. "The Ishmael Reed Image." The Berkeley Gazette,
2 March, p. 9.
McKle reviews Shrovetide in Old New Orleans and finds it
filled with the essays of an artist wishing to communicate
more fully with his readers. She indicates that Shrovetide
"is a book that should be found in the library of anyone
interested in literature, religion, sociology, or world
culture."

18 MARGOLIES, EDWARD, and BAKISH, DAVID, comps. Afro-American
Fiction 1853-1976. Detroit, Mich.: Gale Research Co.,
pp. 101-102.
Consists of bibliographical listings and the briefest
annotations possible on the entire spectrum of material as
indicated in the title. Reed criticism is listed, though
not exhaustively.

19 MAYES, FRANCES. "Scrawling to California: A Poetry of
Place." Bay Guardian Day and Night (16 August):25.
Reviews Calafia and agrees with Bob Callahan, one of its
editors, that it captures the diversity of American culture
as only the State of California has and does. Mayes notes
that Calafia is "a restless history, a restless geog-
raphy . . . given voice."

20 MOORE, PAMELA DENISE. "White Males Dominate American
Society." Spelman Spotlight: The Voice of Black Woman-
hood 32 (April):1.
Reports on Reed's semester as writer-in-residence at
Spelman and briefly touches on his opinions about American
society, publishing, political problems, etc.

21 MUSGRAVE, MARIAN. "Sexual Excess and Deviation as Structural
    Devices in Gunter Grass's Blechtrommel and Ishmael Reed's
    Free-Lance Pallbearers." CLA Journal 22, no. 3 (March):
    229-39.
        Compares Free-Lance Pallbearers and Grass's Blechtrom-
    mel, finding that both authors use the novelistic device
    of superimposing sexual activity in their novels as a
    method of pointing out the deeper societal persecutions.
    Both authors have set their novelistic worlds in periods
    of highly fused prudishness. Musgrave also asserts that
    the underlying structure of Free-Lance Pallbearers is
    hagiographical for its main character Bukka Doopeyduk.

22 PLEASANTS, BEN. "A Poetic Sampling of California Gumbo."
    Los Angeles Times Book Review, 30 September, p. 18.
        Pleasants says that the "point of [Calafia] is to add
    the black, brown, red and yellow voices that have been cut
    away from anthologies too long." The review faults Reed,
    however, for leaving out the "three most important Anglos
    in the state": Gary Snyder, Kenneth Rexroth, and Charles
    Bukowski. But "no matter. Why fight with the cook when
    he's boiling up gumbo." Despite his perceptions of the
    anthology's shortcomings, Pleasants concludes "All in all
    the gumbo is good, though, and it likely will become
    better."

23 REILLY, JOHN M. "The Reconstruction of Genre as Entry into
    Conscious History." Black American Literature Forum 13,
    no. 1 (Spring):3-6.
        Takes up the notion of the novel genre changes which
    are occurring and have occurred through the works of
    Wright, Williams, and Reed. Reilly's major concern is the
    genre of the historical novel which, he points out, was a
    literary reconstruction of objective reality from the on-
    set of the novel genre to at least Wright's Native Son.
    Reed has in each of his novels undertaken "an exercise in
    literary criticism by manipulation of audience expecta-
    tions." Yellow Back Radio Broke-Down "shatters the crys-
    tallized moment of idealized history, . . . normalcy . . .
    the bias of the Western story; Mumbo Jumbo and Last Days
    of Louisiana Red undermine the rationalistic suppositions
    of the detective mystery; . . . Flight to Canada is nothing
    less than revision of the form of the earliest popular
    Afro-American writing, the fugitive slave narrative."
    Reilly concludes: "Without a doubt Reed stretches our
    minds. We must remain constantly aware of his work as
    writing and not permit ourselves the comfort induced by
    old customs of reading that convert literary language into

1979

> a transparent medium through which to glimpse so-called
> objective reality."

24 RHODES, JEWELL PARKER. "Mumbo Jumbo and a Somewhat Private
Literary Response." American Humor: An Interdisciplinary
Newsletter 6:11-13.
> A very personal response to Reed's novel: "Ishmael Reed
> and me have an uneasy alliance. . . . I am now able to
> appreciate that he has been speaking to me for a decade.
> I just wasn't listening properly."

25 SCRUGGS, CHARLES. "Shrovetide in Old New Orleans by Ishmael
Reed." Arizona Quarterly 35, no. 3 (Autumn):275-77.
> Asserts that Shrovetide is "an apologia pro vita sua in
> the guise of a tossed salad," . . . that the "best part
> . . . is the satire," and that "Reed also uses his mis-
> chievous laughter to make some serious observations about
> American society." Scruggs also includes brief comment on
> Reed's entire novel output: "In all of them, Reed sets up
> a dialectical opposition between Western civilization and
> the pagan world which it fears and despises." However,
> Scruggs finds some inconsistencies in Reed's definitions of
> his own satire. "Which is it--muckraker or Osiris? . . .
> Reed finds too many things wrong with America. His 'humor'
> serves his fierce indignation; he is more Juvenal than
> Horace." Scruggs compares Reed's motivation in writing
> "D Hexorcism of Noxon D Awful" with what Jonathan Swift did
> to Robert Walpole in Gulliver's Travels. He concludes:
> "Satire is putting a hex on your enemy, and you don't have
> to go to other cultures to find an explanation for this
> truth."

26 SOUTHGATE, ROBERT L. Black Plots and Black Characters.
Syracuse, N.Y.: Gaylord Professional Publications,
pp. 104, 287, 360.
> Briefly summarizes the plot of Last Days of Louisiana
> Red. Includes brief comment on the plot: "Nothing is what
> it seems to be. . . . Any interpretation would probably be
> invalid, for the reader is never sure whether the joke is
> on him or the author. Reed is a wild, wild writer and a
> skillful one as well."

27 SULLIVAN, THERESA. "Calafia: An Historical Chorus of
California Poets." Inside Art 3 (September-October):2.
> Sullivan refers to Calafia: The California Poetry as
> creating "the colorful gumbo of sound and lyrics, which
> uniquely belongs to the cultural voice of this state." The
> reviewer concludes "so in reading Calafia, open to the

sounds of your California, and don't be surprised if you
hear something you've never heard before."

28 No entry.

29 TUCKER, KEN. "Stirring Poetic Ideals in Calafia (without
    tenure)." Los Angeles Herald Examiner, 22 July, p. E12.
        Depicts Calafia as an "anthology of poetry by 90 writers
    who have made some intimate connection with this state--
    they write about it, live in it, or simply feel it as a
    provoking cultural presence." Tucker points to two themes
    permeating the work throughout: "The first is the crucial
    influence that jazz has had on many poets' ideas of
    cadence and prosody. . . . The other . . . is the sense of
    chummy outlawry these writers feel as they hold their
    creative thumbs in their cultural ears and waggle their
    fingers at the East Coast."

30 TURAN, KENNETH. "Voodoo Man Versus The Moochers." New West
    4 (23 April):63+.
        Amiably touches on the highlights of Reed's career and
    accomplishments so far. "There is bite to almost every-
    thing Ishmael Reed says, a touch of joyous sardonic
    vitriol." Reed speaks of his move to California in 1968:
    "I wanted to come to the most barbarous section of the
    country, where people don't care about literature. I'm
    anonymous here, I get work done."

31 WEIXLMAN, JOE. "Politics, Piracy, and Other Games: Slavery
    and Liberation in Flight to Canada." MELUS 6, no. 3:41-50.
        Offers an explication of the games imagery in the novel.
    He succeeds in bringing to light the gamesmanship of
    Lincoln and the Emancipation Proclamation. He further
    points out that Harriet Stowe stole the plot for Uncle
    Tom's Cabin from Josiah Henson's The Life of Josiah Henson,
    Formerly A Slave and the personal tragedy her gamesplaying
    caused her.

1979

32 WOJACK, ANDREA. "Paperbacks/Ishmael Reed." Detroit News,
    1 March, no pagination.
        Reviewing the paperback edition of Shrovetide in Old
    New Orleans, Wojack finds Reed uncompromising of the prose
    essay. Reed noted that it was "the ditch digging occupa-
    tion" of writing. To this group, Wojack notes that
    "forums like the New York Times and the late Black World
    have been privileged to display some of Reed's more in-
    dustrious shovel work."

                            1980

1   ANON. "Ishmael Reed to Give Poetry Reading, Lecture." The
    Chattanooga (Tenn.) Times, 20 April, p. D10.
        Announcement of Reed's appearance at a poetry reading
    and lecture to raise funds for the Association for the
    Study of Negro Life and History--Roland Hayes Memorial
    Committee, in Chattanooga.

2   ANON. "'Pre-Columbian' Awards." New York Times, 6 March, no
    pagination.
        Announces the honoring of 8 American writers in an
    awards ceremony by The Before Columbus Foundation, which
    was "established four years ago by the novelist Ishmael
    Reed to recognize Afro-American, Asian-American, Mexican-
    American and other writers whose works he believes are
    usually excluded by the established literary tributes."
    Reed said "We think the other book awards are corrupt."

3   BARAKA, AMIRI. "Afro-American Literature and Class Struggle."
    Black American Literature Forum 14, no. 1 (Spring):5-14.
        A lengthy historical review of black literature. At one
    point, Baraka takes Reed to task for upholding the Haitian
    dictatorship of Doc Duvalier.

4   BRYFONSKI, DEDRIA, ed. "Ishmael Reed." In Contemporary Lit-
    erary Criticism. Vol. 13. Detroit, Mich.: Gale Research
    Co., pp. 476-81.
        Reed's portion in this compilation of excerpts from
    critical articles consists of fairly lengthy portions from
    eight articles. The editor introduces Reed's section say-
    ing that he "creates a chaotic fictional world where dogma,
    whether scientific or religious, presents an ominous
    threat. . . . His purpose is to show the sacrifice of
    individuality inherent in accepting any rigid philosophical
    approach to life."

5   FERLINGHETTI, LAWRENCE, and PETERS, NANCY J. Literary San
     Francisco: A Pictorial History from its Beginnings to the
     Present Day. San Francisco: City Lights Books; Harper &
     Row, pp. 219, 230-31.
        Publishes photographs of Ishmael Reed with others who
     participated in the Third San Francisco International
     Poetry Festival as well as photographs of contributors to
     Y-Bird (1979). The caption of the Y-Bird contributors
     mentions Mumbo Jumbo and cites Reed and Al Young as "the
     most potent novelists in the San Francisco area today."
     And "Books like Reed's Mumbo Jumbo put the latest master-
     pieces of Philip Roth, Saul Bellow, John Fowles, and other
     university novelists in the 'deep shade.'" Another photo-
     graph includes the founders of The Before Columbus Founda-
     tion.

6   FOX, THOMAS. "South May Lead U.S. To Justice, Writer Says."
     Memphis (Tenn.) Commercial Appeal, 25 April, no pagination.
        Reports Reed's attendance at a symposium held in
     Memphis, Tennessee.

7   JAMES, CHARLES L. "Reed, Ishmael." In Contemporary Poets.
     Third edition. Edited by James Vinson. New York: St.
     Martin's Press, pp. 1248-50.
        Brief comment. Reed's poems are "not unique in either
     their intent or their responsibility but they are poignant
     examples of the dynamic wit and unabashed approach which
     he demonstrates in his novels."

8   KORWIN-PAWLOWSKA, BETHANY. "Ishmael Reed--Experimental
     Novelist Fighting for Comeback." Oakland Tribune,
     28 September, p. El+.
        A news story announcing the new and upcoming Reed works:
     Quilt, a new magazine, "Personal Problems," a soap opera,
     and Give and Take, a new novel developing around the
     Christmas theme. Space is also devoted to background about
     Reed.

9   _____. "'Personal Problems': New Black Soap Opera." Oakland
     Tribune, 12 December, p. C-3.
        Reports the screening in Berkeley of "Personal Problems,"
     a soap opera which "takes off from script treatments" by
     Reed and Al Young. Reed says "We chose the soap opera
     format because the soap opera is an American invention, and
     for that reason not much has been done to develop it by
     'serious artists.'" The program premiered in Paris at the
     George Pompidou Museum, November 1980.

1980

10   MAYNARD, DORI J. "Poet Thrills Audience." <u>Middlebury Campus</u>,
     20 November, p. 12.
        Discusses Reed's poetry and interview on the campus of
     Middlebury College. "Despite their limited knowledge of
     his work, Reed's listeners were warmly receptive." Various
     comments from Reed are also included regarding his creative
     process, his political beliefs, and his call to technologi-
     cal competence.

11   NAZARETH, PETER. "Ishmael Reed, dir. <u>Calafia: The</u>
     <u>California Poetry</u>." <u>World Literature Today</u> (Summer):no
     pagination.
        Reviews Reed's editorial project, <u>Calafia</u>. Nazareth
     finds the work filled with the poems of the famous, the
     near famous, the anonymous; it depicts a diverse multi-
     cultural environment. He also finds it somewhat uneven,
     says that it is to be expected in an anthology covering
     100 years of writing.

12   WILDERSON, FRANK B., III. "Video Tape Soap Operas." <u>The</u>
     <u>Black Collegian</u> (October/November):190-192.
        Wilderson reviews the problems endemic in black American
     creative efforts on a cooperative basis. He finds the Reed
     production of "Personal Problems" to be shown on cable
     television and will be available through Reed's publishing
     company.

INDEXES

Index to Writings by Ishmael Reed

Index to Writings about Ishmael Reed

Abel, Robert H., 1972.1
Abbott, Ruth, 1976.1
Abbott, Ruth and Simmons, Ira,
    1975.1
Abbot, Steve, 1969.1
Adler, Dick, 1968.1; 1969.2
"Afro American Literature and
    Class Struggle," 1980.3
"Afro-American Poet in New York,
    The," 1971.19
"Afterword [to "When State
    Magicians Fail"], An,"
    1969.23
"'Aint's,' 'Us'ens,' and 'Mother
    Dear': Issues in the Lan-
    guage of Madhubuti, Jones,
    and Reed," 1979.15
Allen, Bruce, 1977.1
"All Stirred up Like Callaloo,"
    1972.34
Ambler, Madge, 1972.2
"American Fiction 1974-1976: The
    People Who Fell to Earth,"
    1978.47
"American Fiction, 1975: Cele-
    bration in Wonderland,"
    1976.56
"American Literature," 1973.20
"Amos and Andy Revisited,"
    1975.48
"Anachronistic Antagonisms,"
    1976.41
". . . and Blacks Fighting for
    Special Identity," 1972.22
Angelou, Maya, 1978.1-2
"Antiwestern in a Black Black
    Vein," 1969.38

Arata, Esther Spring, More Black
    American Playwrights: a
    Bibliography, 1978.8
Armstrong, David, 1975.14;
    1977.13
"Arts in Black America: Ishmael
    Reed, Novelist, The," 1975.40
"Arts in Review--American
    Fiction, 1972: The Void in
    the Mirror," 1973.36
Aubert, Alvin, 1973.9
"Author Sees Slur Against Voodoo
    in 'Exorcist,'" 1974.26
Avant, John Alfred, 1972.13;
    1974.15

Badger, David, 1978.9
Bailey, Leaonead Pack, comp.
    Broadside Authors and
    Artists: An Illustrated
    Biographical Directory,
    1974.16
Bailey, Steve, 1975.15
Bain, Robert, 1979.5
Baker, Houston A., 1975.16-17
Baker, Houston A., Jr., 1972.14
Bannon, Anthony, 1975.18
Bannon, Barbara, 1972.15-16;
    1974.17; 1976.10
Baraka, Amiri, 1980.3
Barber, Peggy, 1977.14
Batchelor, John Calvin, 1976.11;
    1977.15
"Bay Area Author Ishmael Reed,"
    1979.1
Bear Nebula, 1973.10
Beauford, Fred, 1973.11

"Buffalo the Setting of a Wild
Novel," 1976.67
Burns, Jim, 1971.8
Bush, Roland E., 1974.22
"By Ishmael Reed, Surrealist,"
1978.38

Cade, Toni, 1969.10
"Calafia: An Historical Chorus
of California Poets," 1979.27
"Calafia, the California Poetry,"
1979.2
Callahan, Robert et al., 1978.13
"Call Him Ishmael," 1975.22;
1978.28
Campenni, Frank, 1974.23; 1976.20
"'Canada' a Satire of America,"
1976.58
Cannon, Steve, 1977.17
Carr, Audrey, 1971.9
Carter, Albert Howard, III,
1975.21
Carter, Steven R., 1976.21-22
"Casanova's Adventures in Post-
War Germany, A," 1971.1
Cash, Earl A., 1972.19; 1973.15
"Catechism of d Neoamerican
Hoodoo Church," 1971.17-18;
1974.45-46
Chamberlain, E. L., 1977.18
Charyn, Jerome, 1976.23
"Chattanooga," 1973.1, 9; 1974.2,
70
"Chattanooga by Ishmael Reed,"
1973.38
"Chattanooga's Poems," 1974.3
Childs, James, 1969.10
"City in Recent American Litera-
ture: Black on White: A
Study of Selected Writings
of Bellow, Mailer, Ellison,
Baldwin and Writers of the
Black Aesthetic, The,"
1974.33
"Civil War . . . in 'Stereo',
The," 1976.54
"Clarence Major: The Enormous-
ness of Real Art," 1973.12
"Cliché as Archetype, The,"
1969.43

Cohrs, Timothy, 1974.24
Collins, Terence George, 1976.24
Colter, Cyrus, 1974.25
"Comic Historical Novel: Some
Recent Experiments, The,"
1976.72
"Comic Modes in Black America,"
1978.44
"Compassionate View," 1971.28
"Conjure," 1972.4; 1973.2, 26
"Conjure: Selected Poems, 1963-
1970," 1972.17
"Conjure by Ishmael Reed,"
1973.27
"Conjuring With Words," 1978.23
Connell, Chris, 1974.26-27
"Contemporary American Writer
and His Sense of Ethnicity--
Or Is the Fishing Better in
Your Own River?, The,"
1975.41
"Contentious State of the
Language, The," 1979.11
Contoski, Victor, 1979.7
"Conversation with Ishmael Reed,"
1973.11
Cooper, Arthur, 1975.22
"Cosmic Myth, A," 1972.42
Courlandar, Harold, 1976.25
Crabbe, Ken, 1969.11
Crawley, Phillip, 1971.10
"Creative, Unique, Personal
View," 1976.31
Crouch, Stanley, 1979.8
"Cultural Nationalism in Afro-
American Literature,"
1972.23
"Cultures Clash in Mumbo Jumbo,"
1972.31

Dalke, Jeff, 1974.28
Darling, Lynn, 1969.12
Davis, Arthur P., 1978.14
-From the Dark Tower: Afro-
American Writers 1900-1960,
1974.29
Davis, George, 1972.20-21
"Decline and Fall of Jes Grew,"
1972.32

"Ishmael Reed Raises Questions
About Abe Lincoln's
Identity," 1976.11
"Ishmael Reed Returning for U/B
Modern Lit Event," 1975.3
"Ishmael Reed Spices Language
with 'Gumbo,'" 1976.18
"Ishmael Reed's Canada," 1977.40
"Ishmael Reed's Defiant Voice,"
1978.37
"Ishmael Reed's Flight to
Canada," 1977.16
"Ishmael Reed's Free-Lance
Pallbearers: On the
Dialectics of Shit," 1977.24
"Ishmael Reed's Mumbo-Jumbo
Literary Gumbo," 1975.23
"Ishmael Reed's NeoHooDoo
Detection," 1976.21-22
"Ishmael Reed's Yardbird Press,"
1977.13
"Ishmael Reed to Give Poetry
Reeding, Lecture," 1980.1
"It's That New Black 'HooDoo,'"
1974.69
Ivie, Ardie, 1976.41
Iwamoto, Iwao Gendai no
American Shosetsu: Tairitsu
to Mosaku, 1974.39

Jackson, Blyden and Rubin,
Louis D., Jr. Black Poetry
in America: Two Essays in
Historical Interpretation,
1974.40
Jackson, David, 1979.13
Jackson, Leandre, 1975.27
Jacob, Walter, 1979.14
Jacobs, Theodore J., 1972.29
James, Charles L., 1975.28;
1980.7
Jefferson, Margo, 1976.42
"Jess Grew Threatens Uptight
America," 1972.33
Johnson, Herschel, 1973.25
Johnson, Lemuel A., 1979.15
Jones, Earl A., 1977.27
Jones, Robert W., 1978.32
Joye, Barbara, 1968.4
"Joyfully Erudite Look at
America," 1976.32

Katz, Bill, 1971.14
Katz, William and Richards,
Berry G. Magazines for
Libraries, 1978.34
Katzman, Allan, 1967.7-8; 1969.29
Kaiser, Ernest, 1974.41; 1978.33
Keiya, 1978.35
Kent, George E., 1975.29; 1978.36
Kimball, George, 1968.5
Kinnamon, Keneth, 1967.9
Klinkowitz, Jerome, 1974.42;
1976.43
-The Life of Fiction, 1977.28
-Literary Disruptions: The
Making of a Post-Contemporary
American Fiction, 1975.30
Klotman, Phyllis Rauch. Another
Man Gone: The Black Runner
in Contemporary Afro-American
Literature, 1977.29
Kohl, Herb, 1977.30
Korwin-Pawlowska, Bethany,
1980.8-9
Kostelanetz, Richard. The End
of Intelligent Writing:
Politics in America, 1974.43
"KPFA Poetry Festival, The,"
1977.4

Lamming, George, 1973.26
Landry, Donna, 1976.44
Lane, George, 1972.30
"Language and Structure in
Ishmael Reed's Yellow Back
Radio Broke-Down," 1978.32
Larson, Charles R., 1977.31;
1978.37
"Last Days of Louisiana Red,"
1974.7-11, 15, 59; 1975.4-5,
17, 25, 50
"Last Days of Louisiana Red by
Ishmael Reed, The," 1975.16
Le Clair, Thomas, 1976.45
Lee, Christopher Herron, 1975.31
Lee, Deborah, 1973.27
Lee, Robert, 1972.31
Lehmann-Haupt, Christopher,
1969.30; 1972.32-33; 1974.44
Leshkol, Abraham, 1967.10
Lester, Julius, 1970.9